Apples & Man

Apples & Man

Fred Lape

Drawings by Phyllis Wood

 Van Nostrand Reinhold Company
New York Cincinnati Toronto London Melbourne

Copyright © 1979 by Litton Educational Publishing, Inc.
Library of Congress Catalog Card Number 78-10682
ISBN 0-442-24678-1

Designed by Loudan Enterprises
Drawings by Phyllis Wood

Published in 1979 by Van Nostrand Reinhold Company
A division of Litton Educational Publishing, Inc.
135 West 50th Street, New York, NY 10020, U.S.A.

Van Nostrand Reinhold Limited
1410 Birchmount Road
Scarborough, Ontario M1P 2E7, Canada

Van Nostrand Reinhold Australia Pty. Ltd.
17 Queen Street
Mitcham, Victoria 3132, Australia

Van Nostrand Reinhold Company Limited
Molly Millars Lane
Wokingham, Berkshire, England

16 15 14 13 12 11 10 9 8 7 6 5 4 3 2 1

Library of Congress Cataloging in Publication Data
Lape, Fred, 1900-
    Apples and man.
    Includes index.
    1. Apple.   I. Title.
SB363.L36   634'.11   78-10682
ISBN 0-442-24678-1

634
Lape

Acknowledgments

Portions of Chapter 3 appeared in slightly different form in *Arnoldia* and *The New York Times* and are used here with the permission of The Arnold Arboretum of Harvard University and The New York Times © 1975 by The New York Times Company. Portions of Chapters 3, 5, and 8 appeared in slightly different form in *Organic Gardening* and are used here with the permission of Rodale Press Inc.

Contents

1. The Genus *Malus*

The apple, like wheat, rose with the dawn of man. It is a European fruit and, like European culture, has spread around the world. Its origins are mysterious; its early mentions enigmatic. Were the Golden Apples of the Hesperides apples? Probably not, for the apple was not a common fruit of Greece. "As the apple tree among the trees of the wood, so is my beloved among the sons," sings the singer of the Canticles in the Bible, but it probably was not an apple tree, for the apple is not a Palestinian fruit. The first English translations of the Bible were made in a north country. The apple was the fruit of England. The Hebrew *tappauch*, a generic word for fruit, including the orange, the peach, the quince, and the apricot, became an apple, the delight of the English dairy maid.

The best indications are that the apple began first to be domesticated in the region just south of the Caucasus, but even by prehistoric times it had spread all over Europe from the Caspian Sea to the Atlantic Ocean. Charred remains of apples have been found in the mud, prehistoric lake dwellings near Switzerland. The apple spread west first, rather than east, and arrived only late beyond the Gobi Desert. It is found wild in the mountains of northwest India but not in Japan, Mongolia, or Siberia. There were species of apples native to China and Japan, but they were all of the type we know as crabapples, inedible raw. This seems to be the only apple known in early China. Not until after the Middle Ages, when European culture first reached the Far East, did the large edible apple arrive there.

From its early sources it spread wherever man spread; for the apple, like the starling and the English sparrow, is a readily adaptable form of life. Its gene pool is rich. It yields to infinite variation, both in fruit and in the adaptability of the plant to climatic conditions. The orange and the cocoanut palm have spread around the tropic belt but never have adapted themselves to the temperate zone. The apple has invaded the tropics, where it will fruit if given sufficient elevation and a dormant rest period. It has become almost as common as the orange in the markets of Mexico.

It takes a remarkably short time for the apple to become established in a region. It grows readily from seed. Throw the core of an apple on fertile ground, and in a few years there will be an apple tree. The only apples native to North America were, as in eastern Asia, crabapples. North European settlers brought apples with them. Only a hundred years later the Iroquois Indians, an intelligent group, had made the apple their own, so much so that when in the years of the Revolutionary War General Sullivan led an expedition against the Cayugas and Senecas, he found apple orchards bending with fruit. In the early years of this century two old apple trees remained of the old Indian orchards near the Geneva Experimental Station in New York State.

Botanically the apple belongs to the Rosaceae, the great family of the roses, which includes not only apples, peaches, pears, plums, and raspberries, but such dissimilar plants as spireas and the mountain ash. In the temperate climate of the United States, there are over forty genera of the Rosaceae. In the history of plant life it is one of the earlier developed families, the flowers of which are relatively regular and simple. Today, botanists have agreed to call the apple genus *Malus,* but a century ago it was lumped with the pear into a genus *Pyrus,* the apple being distinguished as *Pyrus malus.*

As of all plants that have been domesticated for centuries, it is difficult to say now whether the simple ancestor of the apple still exists. There are two wild apples of Europe, *Malus pumila* and *Malus sylvestris,* but are they actually ancestors, or are they merely stable hybrids remaining after centuries of wild seeding? It becomes particularly complicated when one realizes that a variety of *Malus pumila, M. p. niedzwetskyana,* a small apple red to the core with red flowers, has led in the last hundred years under hybridization with the Asiatic crabapples to a tremendous number of red-leaved and red- or magenta-flowering ornamental crabapples. If this much hybridization can happen in a few generations, one is hesitant to generalize too specifically about the past three or four thousand years.

The reason that apples and pears were for a long time lumped together under the genus *Pyrus* is that the botanical distinction between the two is slight. The styles of the pear flower—that is, the stems of the pistils—are free and separate at the base; the styles of the apple flower are united at the base. One can also make a couple of loose generalizations, such as that all pear blossoms are white and apple blossoms run a gamut of color from white to dark red, almost purple, and that the shape of the fruit is distinctive. The fact is that there are almost round pears and almost pear-shaped apples. The pears are more southern, originating from the Mediterranean peninsula; the apples, more northern. Even the Latin word *malus,* from which the genus is named, meant only a large fruit tree, and did not come to mean an apple tree until later.

Although there is presently an active search among botanists to trace the origins of all genera of plants, no intricate study, as far as I know, has been made of the genus *Malus*. The American species present a problem. All of the native American species are small trees with small, green, sour fruit, commonly known as crabapples. From what we know of the migration of peoples and plants to the Western Hemisphere, it would seem as though the species came across the Bering Straits, along with the man migrations. Why then are there six or more species confined to the eastern half of the United States and only one on the west coastal slope between the Rockies and the Pacific? Why, in fact, is there so little resemblance between the Asiatic and the American crabapples? Was there perhaps a more distant source of the American species in that far north country, now arctic but once semitropic according to fossil proof, from which they may have advanced down into America in front of the glaciers?

The word apple has the same stem among the Celts, Germans, Lithuanians, and Slavs, and this indicates the sections of Europe where the greatest development of the edible apple occurred. The word has no classical source. It only becomes a synonym of the Latin *malus* after interchange by conquest and trade with the northern tribes of Europe.

It is the richness of the gene pool of the genus *Malus* that has led to the infinite variety of apples that have come and gone in the past four centuries. All of the species hybridize readily, from the tiny fruited *Malus sieboldii* of Japan to the Northern Spy of New York and Ontario. Plant the seed of a small sour apple, and you may get among the seedlings a large sweet apple, the reappearance of a strain years buried in the past of the small sour apple.

It was not until the discovery of propagation by grafting and budding that one could count on any single variety lasting longer than the lifetime of the tree upon which it grew, for scarcely any variety of apple comes true from seed. The dwarf *Malus sargenti*, the Sargent crabapple of Japan, though, seems to be an exception to this, and a few strains of edible apples transmit their qualities fairly well when seeded from a female parent of the strain.

It is fascinating to guess how the process of grafting was first discovered. Was it perhaps by the chance union of two branches of a tree rubbing against each other and eventually growing together and some observant early man thinking, why not two different branches brought together? However and whenever the first try, it was a well-developed method of propagation by the time of Greece and Rome.

It was not only the apple's versatility and prolific seeding that made it follow man's steps over the earth. More than any other fruit except the grape, the apple endeared itself to men from the beginning. The beauty and fragrance of its blossoms, the beauty of its fruit, and the fragrance and taste of its fruit all moved their way into the folklore, the sayings, and the speech of all groups who cultivated it. In the index to *Bartlett's Familiar Quotations*, there are forty-six quotations about the apple, only six about the orange. The apple appears in the mythology of all the northern European countries. In Scandinavia Iduna, daughter of the dwarf Svald and wife of Bragi, kept in a box the apples that the gods tasted as often as they wished to renew their youth. Down to the middle of the last century, a custom prevailed in Devonshire and Herefordshire, the English apple sections, of a yearly salute to the apple trees in order to insure a good harvest. The farmer and his sons gathered around a tree with a wassail bowl of hard cider and some pieces of toast in it. They poured a little of the cider about the roots of the tree, hung pieces of wet toast on barren branches, and after drinking the rest of the cider, danced around the tree and sang a song of fertility.

> Hail to thee, good apple tree,
> Well to bear pocket-fuls, hat-fuls,
> Peck-fuls, bushel-bag-fuls . . .

The use of toast in such ceremonies was the origin of our use of the word toast as a salute. Here in New England when little girls were peeling apples, they tossed a long curl of apple peeling over their shoulders to see what letter—the initial of their future lover—it would make when it fell. They also marked apple seeds with initials and stuck the seeds to their foreheads; the seed that stuck longest bore the initials of the future husband.

The Romans, good horticulturists, brought their varieties of apples to England, but the later Normans seem to have been the more active introducers, for many of the early English apples bear Gallic names. Whatever the source, there were by 1688 seventy-eight varieties in cultivation in the neighborhood of London, and by 1900 the number had grown to two thousand. Actually, the breeding source of the modern apple lies more on the continent: northern France, Holland, Germany, and Russia.

However, one can almost say that the fruition of the apple came when it reached North America, for in the northeastern United States and southeastern Canada it found the warm summers and the cold winters suited to its perfect development. Perhaps the cold winters were the most important, for always the best tasting apples have come from the northern end of its ranges at the very limit of easy endurance of cold winters. It was not long after the settlement of Rhode Island that the Rhode Island Greening appeared there. In northern New England, New York, Quebec, and Ontario have appeared a series of varieties, usually chance seedlings, that have for nearly two centuries set the standard of taste for the modern apple.

During the early decades of the Northeast, no farm was complete without its apple orchard, sweet with blossoms in spring, the hollow trees forming nesting sites for flickers and bluebirds. Birds and rodents carried away the excess fruit with its seeds to start new hybrids.

Anyone who has lived in apple country that is also farmland knows how young apple trees spring up everywhere in land that is not cultivated. In old cow pastures they struggle for years against the constant grazing of their leaves by cows, until their base is an elongated mound of stubby branches with a mat of leaves deep inside where a cow's tongue cannot reach. Sometimes one manages to get a branch above the reach of a cow's neck and jaws, and from then on its growth is easier. Later, when it bears fruit, the cows cluster around its base at fruiting time, nibbling the fallen apples. Sometimes these seedlings have good fruit. When I was a boy, we had two trees in our cow pasture from which we always picked the fruit and brought it to the cellar to store. One bore a bright red apple that made pies almost as good as those of Red Astrachan. The other bore an almost white sweet apple with a pink cheek, delicious for eating out of hand. Nobody thought to make grafts from either tree, and both are long dead, varieties that might, who knows, have become famous if propagated and publicized.

The place to look for wild apple thickets was along the steep banks of small streams, where no cows grazed to trouble them when young. There, wild apple trees often grew in profusion, the branches of varieties mingled in their slim tops. The fruit was of all colors and all sizes, many so sour they puckered the mouth and some woody and dry with scarcely any taste at all. In early winter the ground would be littered with them.

Thoreau knew these wild apples in his walks around Concord. He sampled them all. There were a couple of trees whose fruit he found particularly delicious in December and January after they had been frozen and lay on the ground under the snow. It must have been the fruit of such a tree that later led schoolboys from a farm section in Pennsylvania in April of the next spring to a tree that was propagated and is still popular under the name of York Imperial.

These wild seedlings varied too with their flowers. I remember some of them that opened and faded rose pink, darker than all their neighbors. I have often wondered why none of these wild varieties were ever propagated and grown for ornamentals or hybridized for even darker colored flowers. Now, however, the hybrids of the Asiatic crabapples and of the red-flowered *Malus pumila niedzwetskyana* have become common ornamentals, and these probably have better genes for flower color than any wild apple seedlings.

Another advantage of the rich gene pool of the apple has been its ability to develop in each geographical area where it has advanced new varieties particularly adaptable to survival in that region and with a distinctive taste. Such would be the Red Astrachan in Russia, the Northern Spy and the Spitzenburg in New York, the Bellflower in New Jersey, the Smokehouse in Pennsylvania, and the Delicious in Iowa. The Northern Spy, when grown in Virginia, ripens earlier and loses both the tang of its flavor and its keeping quality, but a few varieties have proved successful when grown in a new region. The Bellflower became a superior apple in California; the Delicious found its home in Washington.

By now the apple has spread far beyond Europe and North America, but it has, in general, followed the north European emigrants. Since the apple was not well suited to the climate of Spain, the Spaniards paid little attention to it. The pear and the orange were their fruits, and it was their seeds that the Spanish padres carried with them when they founded missions up the western coast into what is now California. Their old pear trees are still sometimes found growing in the old mission gardens. It remained for the New Englanders and the Iowans, all north European stock, to bring the apple to California after the gold rush. It was probably not the Spaniards but the Germans who carried the apple to South America, particularly to the Argentine, and obviously, the English who carried it to Australia and New Zealand, where it has been able to adjust itself not only to a strange climate but to a complete reversal of its natural seasons of growth.

A remarkable genus, *Malus*.

2. The Spread of the Apple in North America

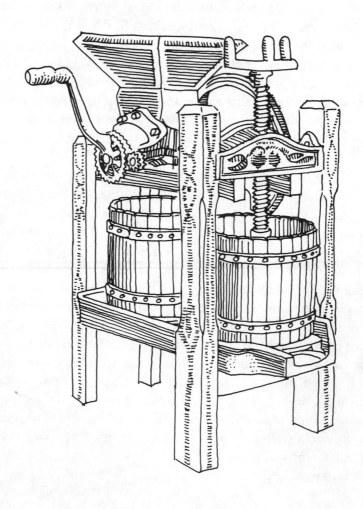

John Endicott, an early governor of Massachusetts, is said to have brought the first apple tree to America. This would have been in the early 1600s. Many of the early English colonists brought seeds and plants with them from Europe. So did the early French settlers in Quebec. Since it was obvious from the start that the edible apple of Europe had found a home as fertile for development as the settlers themselves were finding, apple trees soon became a feature of early settlements.

It soon became obvious, too, that the apple was important economically in early colonial life. No apples were wasted. Those that were not eaten raw or cooked or stored in cellars for winter eating or preserved over winter by drying, were crushed and squeezed for cider. In fact, the production of cider became one of the most important uses of the fruit, and a variety that was good for cider was often as popular as a variety that was good for eating.

The economic value of cider was fourfold: as a delightful fresh drink; as an equally delightful mild alcoholic drink in the form of hard cider; as a potent alcoholic drink in the form of applejack, an apple brandy made by freezing rather than by distilling; and finally, as vinegar. The importance of the apple for cider and vinegar persisted during the first two centuries of America under north European colonization. Most farms had a small cider press in which the excess of the farm apple crop was turned to cider and later to vinegar. Every small village had its cider mill operating during the late summer and fall. Farmers brought their excess apples to the mill in lumber wagons. The cider was stored in barrels in the cellars. The faintly acid-sweet smell of the apple pulp behind the cider mill was, even as late as the early 1900s, a common fragrance, nostalgic now to remember.

Not only locally, but in world trade the apple soon attained economic importance. The first actual record of trade in apples to the West Indies is in 1740, but the trade had probably begun long before this. Early too there came a demand for American apples in Europe, particularly in England.

In spite of this brisk trade, commercial apple orchards did not develop until late. Also, the spread of native American varieties was very gradual. Since it was much easier to bring apple seeds from Europe than to bring growing plants, most of the early orchards were merely seedling trees; not more than five to ten percent of the trees were of grafted stock. Some of the seedling trees bore excellent fruit, others mediocre. For the economy of the period this was not important. An apple that was of little use for eating might be an excellent apple for cider, and if it was too flavorless to be valuable even for cider, it was at least good fodder for the pigs, which every farmer, and indeed most villagers, raised.

In general, the spread of better varieties followed the establishment of nurseries. The importance of the early nurseries in the colonies and subsequently in the whole United States cannot be ignored. Not only did they disseminate new varieties of fruits, but they were also the botanical gardens of their day. John Bartram's garden on the banks of the Schuylkill in Philadelphia and Robert Prince's nursery on Long Island were for their period what the Arnold Arboretum or the Bronx Botanical Garden were for the late 1800s. The Prince nursery was started in 1730. The Huguenots, who had settled at New Rochelle and on the north shore of Long Island, had brought with them a variety of French fruits, and this created an interest in fruit development. Already by 1815 Prince was offering many varieties of grafted apples, and his catalog of 1845 contains 350 varieties. By this time commercial orchards were well on their way and most were planting grafted trees and sorting out the better varieties. By this time too, nurseries were developing in western New York State, in Rochester, Geneva, and Dansville. This area was to vie with the lower Hudson Valley as the most productive apple orchard area in the United States, until that distinction passed to the Northwest. Across the Appalachians already nurseries were springing up in Ohio and what was later to be Iowa.

Much has been made of the legend of Johnny Appleseed as the distributor of apples from the eastern seaboard to the Midwest, but we should not let legend obscure fact. Johnny Appleseed did not leave Pennsylvania for Ohio until 1800, and the earliest record of the planting of an apple tree in what was later to be Iowa was a tree planted by one Julien Dubuque before 1795. Also, one Louis Honoré Tesson planted an apple orchard near the present Montrose, Iowa, in 1799. Settlers moving in from the east too brought apple trees or seeds. The beginning in Iowa was important, for during the middle 1800s, Iowa became an important center of apple development. Iowa State University at Ames was one of the earliest in the United States to have an important horticultural course. It was from Iowa that the apple was first brought to Oregon and the Northwest, an area that was later to vie with New York State as the center of apple production in the United States.

And Johnny Appleseed? Born in Leominster, Massachusetts, on September 26, 1774, he was of the generation of the individualists. He must have been a rather precocious young man, for by the time he was twenty-five, then living in Pennsylvania, he had become a Swedenborgian. Evidently life in the East dissatisfied him, for in 1800 he started down the Ohio River with a boat load of apple seeds from the cider mills of Pennsylvania. He was, in a way, an early counterpart of the modern hippie. In place of modern beads and a guru gown, he wore, according to legend, a coffee sack for a shirt and a saucepan for a hat. Wherever he went, he scattered some of his apple seeds, and whenever he could find a listener, he read aloud from the Bible he always carried with him and preached the Swedenborgian doctrine.

He seems to have been a natural friend to almost anything and anybody; birds, animals, settlers, and Indians. The Indians of Ohio thought he was a medicine man, and he helped them when he could. He was always ready to save anybody from disaster. He often warned the Indians when the settlers were planning an attack on them, but equally, in 1812 when he learned that the Indians were about to raid the village of Mansfield, Ohio, he made his way through the forest by night to Mt. Vernon, thirty-six miles away, and brought troops to defend the town.

Always a wanderer, in the 1830s he moved out of Ohio to northern Indiana. He died in Allen County, Indiana, in March of 1845. Presumably, he left a trail of apple seedlings behind him wherever he went. It must be remembered, however, that all of the section through which he passed was being rapidly settled by eastern farmers who often brought with them their favorite apples or young plants and that already a few infant nurseries were appearing in the area.

The movement of the apple from the Midwest to the Far West was more difficult. The distance was longer, the country to be passed through was arid and less hospitable, and the prairie schooner was still the only conveyance.

In the late 1830s one Henderson Lewelling had established a large fruit nursery at Salem in Henry County, Iowa, profitable enough that he could build himself an imposing yellow limestone house. Lewelling, like Johnny Appleseed, was a natural wanderer. He began to hear tales of the fertility of the Willamette Valley in Oregon, and by 1845 he decided to close out his Iowa nursery and move to Oregon. In the spring of 1847 he built a special covered wagon with two boxes filled with a compost of charcoal and earth set in the bottom. Into these he set his stock to be moved: grafted young apple trees, pears, quinces, plums, cherries, grapes, and berries, about seven hundred plants in all from twenty inches to four feet high. He also laid in a stock of fruit seeds. On April 17 of that year with seven wagons in his party, he, a partner, and his family set out for Oregon. Beyond the Missouri the little party joined a wagon train, the common arrangement for safety.

Lewelling's traveling nursery was an impediment to the wagon train. The wagon loaded with nursery stock was heavy. It moved slowly. The plains were hot. The oxen grew lame. Somewhere along the Sweetwater River, Lewelling's partner died, probably from cholera, the scourge of the plains crossings. Two of Lewelling's oxen died. Irritation grew among the other wagons in the train because the men felt that Lewelling's load was holding the train back. They implored him to throw away the nursery stock, saying he would never be able to get it over the mountains anyway. Lewelling refused, but in the end he had to leave the train and travel alone with his seven wagons.

He watered his trees every day, no matter how scarce the

water. Half of the young trees had died, but the rest were in full leaf, and these actually once saved the lives of the small party, for when a band of Indians attacked, the Indians, amazed at the green growth in the one schooner, concluded that the party must be under the special care of the Great Spirit and withdrew.

In October Lewelling reached The Dalles in Oregon, transferred his goods to a boat, and floated down the Columbia River. On November 17, seven months after leaving Iowa, he reached the Willamette Valley, settled his family in a squatter's cabin, transferred to the soil the nursery stock left in his boxes, some of which had grown three feet more in height on the way, and planted the seeds he had brought with him.

By 1851 the young orchard he had planted began to bear fruit. In the meantime he had been propagating from his stock, and was already running a prosperous nursery and selling plants to the Oregon settlers. In 1853 he took his summer crop of apples to San Francisco and sold them for a dollar a pound. He had been joined by his brother Seth, and with Seth's financial acumen the business prospered.

There was also an unexpected bonanza. Among the seeds that Lewelling had brought with him had been some cherry pits, and among the seedlings from these appeared a cherry tree with delicious fruit, large and dark colored, nearly black. Seth propagated the variety and named it after a Chinese workman called Bing. It was to become, and remains even today, the most popular cherry of the Far West.

The nursery was now an assured success. Lewelling was rich, but he was still a wanderer at heart. He was tired of Oregon. He moved to California, founded the town of Fruitvale, planted another orchard, and founded another nursery. He was as successful here as always before. Then the wandering fever hit him again. He heard tales of the splendid opportunities in Honduras. He sold his property in Fruitvale, bought a ship, recruited a band of colonists, and sailed to Honduras.

This was the beginning of the end. He was inexperienced in tropical agriculture and went broke. He returned to California an old and disappointed man. He started another fruit orchard, but the spirit had gone out of him. Competition was strong, and he was no longer a pioneer. He died poorer than when he had set out from Iowa.

Henderson Lewelling's story is a melodrama, but it shows the movement of the apple from Iowa to Oregon and California. A less dramatic story, but one perhaps more typical, is that of Tobias Miller, who came from Jasper County, Iowa, in 1874 and homesteaded eighty acres of land on Sardine Creek, near Gold Hill, Oregon. By this time the covered-wagon days were over. One could travel by train across the Rockies and the desert, and the transport of young trees was a different matter. How many of the trees in Tobias Miller's orchard he brought with him and how many he bought from local nurseries is not known for sure. What is known is that Miller knew a good apple when he tasted one, for among the trees in his orchard were: the Snow, this probably from Quebec; the King, the large showy red apple from New York State; the Northern Spy; the Red Astrachan; the Yellow Transparent; the Spitzenburg; the Rhode Island Greening; and the Gravenstein. It is a list of which any orchardist might be proud.

Tobias Miller was no wanderer. He spent the rest of his life on his homesteaded farm, and now one-hundred years later his orchard still remains. If Oregon has not in the last one hundred years produced new and exciting apples, it is not for lack of good breeding stock.

The same is true of Washington. In 1904 the Baldwin, the Rhode Island Greening, the Esopus Spitzenburg, and the Yellow Bellflower were all growing there.

What is the variety for which the Northwest is now best known? The Delicious, a far step downward from any of the varieties just mentioned. Here we run up against a development that bodes ill for the cultivated apple.

3. O Rare Northern Spy

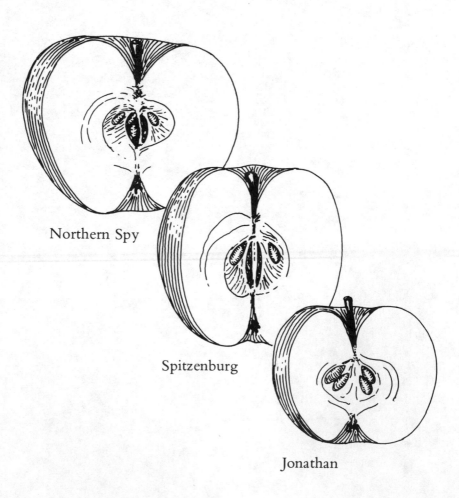

Northern Spy

Spitzenburg

Jonathan

If, as it seems, the climate of northeastern North America offered the developing genus *Malus* a perfection of taste that in all its previous centuries of development it had not attained, then there are sad indications at the present that the species *Homo sapiens* was not wise enough to preserve the perfection achieved. There are indications now that the great peak of apple history, that climax of flavor of the period 1790–1900, may soon be a thing of the past, and that a youth of a hundred years from now may never know the unique taste of a superior apple.

The development of the apple by man in the twentieth century has been partially a retrogression. This is a strange paradox, for exactly in this time the breeding of new varieties of apples has been taken over from chance to scientific planning in agricultural experiment stations. The trouble is that the breeding programs have been geared almost completely to commercial interests. The criteria for selection of new varieties have been an apple that will keep well under refrigeration, ship well without bruising, and have a luscious color which will attract the housewife to buy it from a supermarket, and whose tree will produce a heavy crop annually. That the taste of these selected apples is inferior has been ignored. As a result, sharpness and variety of flavor are disappearing. The apple is becoming as standardized to mediocrity as the average manufactured product. As small farms with their own orchards dwindle and the average person is forced to eat only apples raised by commercial growers, the coming generation will scarcely know how a good apple tastes.

This is not to say that all of the old varieties were good. Many of them were as inferior as a Rome Beauty or a red Delicious, but the best ones were of an excellence that has almost disappeared.

As a standard of excellence by which to judge, I would set the Northern Spy as the best apple ever grown in the United States. To bite into the tender flesh of a well-ripened Spy and have its juice ooze around the teeth and its rich tart flavor fill the mouth and its aroma rise up into the nostrils is one of the outstanding experiences of all fruit eating. More than this, the

Spy is just as good cooked as when eaten raw. In pies and applesauce it holds its firmness and its flavor.

I speak of the Northern Spy in the present because it is still being sold, usually at top prices, at the older orchards in the Northeast. One can buy it occasionally in the larger cities, at special stores and exorbitant prices. It is still being planted by commercial orchards but in small quantities. According to the *New York Orchard and Vineyard Survey* it is twelfth on the list of varieties planted from 1965 to 1970 in New York State commercial orchards, and New York State produces about one-fifth of the apples grown in the United States. Twelfth means 25,000 trees planted, against 150,000 of an inferior tasting variety like Idared, and 60,000 of the woody Delicious. I no longer see it on the shelves of the supermarkets. Definitely, its production is declining rapidly.

There is reason for this. The Northern Spy tree is large and difficult to keep in shape for picking. It is slow to come into bearing, sometimes taking up to fourteen years, although this is unusual. The tree tends to be a biennial bearer of full crops. Since the skin of the fruit is thin and tender, special care must be used in handling. The fruit is also susceptible to a wireworm, which writes tiny scrolls of brown through the flesh and gives it a bitter taste. Also, the fruit on under limbs are shaded from the sun and have less color and sometimes inferior taste to those on exposed branches. Such is the price one pays for perfection, but the Northern Spy is worth it.

The Northern Spy is purely an American apple. It was a seedling in an orchard at East Bloomfield, New York, planted by Heman Chapin from seeds brought from Salisbury, Connecticut, in the year 1800. It is thought that one parent may have been the Wagener. The original tree died before bearing, but one Roswell Humphrey had taken sprouts from the base, and from these sprouts nine trees survived and were still living in 1847. So there was drama in its beginning, so close did it come to being lost. For a few years the variety was confined to the vicinity of its origin, but by 1840 it had begun to attract general attention, and by 1852 the American Pomological Society listed it as a variety worthy of general cultivation.

After that time its fame spread rapidly throughout the Northeast.

It is a large apple with a thin, tender skin and juicy, tart yellow flesh. It ripens late, and then the color is a dull yellow streaked with bright red. It is typical of the breeding programs of this century that in some orchards the Northern Spy has been replaced by the Red Northern Spy, which has the brilliant red skin that our generation seems to feel is so essential in an apple but only a shadow of the taste of the old Northern Spy.

My other standard of excellence has almost disappeared. It is the Spitzenburg, originally known as the Esopus Spitzenburg because it originated at Esopus in Ulster County, New York. Its date of origin is not known, but by 1900 it was considered an old apple throughout New York State. In my childhood no farm orchard would be without one Spitzenburg tree. My most vivid memory of the orchard on our farm was the old Spitzenburg tree, hollow in its upper core, with a hole where the flickers nested each spring when the tree was pink in flower, and hanging red with fruit in October, like a jewel among the other trees.

The fruit is medium size, semiconic in shape but not long, and somewhat ribbed. The skin is a deep, rich yellow verging into bright red and flaming red marked by pale yellow dots at its best. The flesh is tinged with yellow and is firm, crisp, tender, and aromatic but not as juicy as that of the Northern Spy. The taste is unique, as good in its way as the taste of the Northern Spy. Like the Spy, it is as good cooked as when eaten raw, a criterion of goodness by which few apple varieties qualify. In our neighborhood it was always considered the supreme apple for baking.

A few commercial orchards still have an old tree or two tucked away in a corner. Some twenty years ago, when I was in my fifties, I went to one of these orchards to get some Spitzenburg scions for grafting. The owner of the orchard turned me over to his father, whom I judged to be in his eighties, to show me the tree. On the way I tried to make conversation by saying I thought the Spitzenburg was a pretty good apple, whereupon the old gentleman turned in his tracks, looked at me severely, and said, "Young man, the Spitzenburg is the best apple God ever invented."

In recent years I have heard of no new commercial plantings. The Jonathan, one seedling of the Spitzenburg, is smaller and redder than the Spitzenburg but not as inferior to the Spitzenburg as the Red Northern Spy is to the Northern Spy. It has proved itself adaptable to more southern climates as well as to the climate of the Northeast.

The original tree grew on the farm of Philip Rick of Kingston, New York, was described first by a Judge Buel, and was named by him after one Jonathan Hasbrouck, who first called the fruit to his attention. It was perhaps the bright red color of the fruit which sent the variety on its long road to fame, for it is now known all over the world. Its value in New York State is testified by the fact that one maker of commercial applesauce in the western part of the state uses primarily Jonathans, and this applesauce is the best commercial applesauce I have eaten. From New York it spread to the south and to the west, and in later years it has gone to Europe, where it is frequently listed among the top varieties; to Australia, where it is now second on the list of production; and even to Japan. It has been and continues to be used in breeding programs. Many of the modern varieties coming out of agricultural experiment stations have Jonathan in their ancestry.

I have pondered about the success of the Jonathan over the Spitzenburg. To me the Spitzenburg has a slight edge on flavor, and it is a larger apple. Can it be merely that red color of the Jonathan that has sealed its success? I recently asked one of the plant breeders at the Agricultural Experiment Station in Geneva, New York, which has used the Jonathan in several crosses, why the Spitzenburg had not been used more. He said that they had tried it, but the populations did not show good promise; however, the Idaho Agricultural Experiment Station has produced one new variety, Idagold, by crossing the Spitzenburg with Wagener. This is well recommended, but I have not tasted it. Obviously, there are possibilities yet in the Spitzenburg, and the Spitzenburg should not be lost as a gene source, but the Jonathan itself is close to its parent, and one cannot complain of it, since it has succeeded in making the Spitzenburg strain one of the perhaps four leading strains in modern apple breeding.

I suppose that if one were to give a prize to the variety that has managed to hold its own for the longest time in competition with other varieties, that prize would have to go to the Rhode Island Greening, more commonly called the Greening. It originated in the 1700s in Rhode Island, near Newport, at a place known as Green's End, where a Mr. Green kept a tavern and raised apple trees from seed. The fruit from the original tree was occasionally given to visitors at the tavern. The visitors who came back in succeeding springs asking for grafting scions from the tree started the Greening on its two centuries of success. Its fame soon spread throughout the northeast. It is a long-lived, sturdy, wide-spreading tree. One tree cut down in 1903 was known to be nearly two-hundred years old.

The fruit is large, the skin grass green varying to dull yellow, sometimes with a cinnamon blush on the sun side. I cannot for excellence put it in the class of the Northern Spy or the Spitzenburg, for it is inferior to both when eaten raw, but in many households of the Northeast it still reigns supreme as a cooking apple. It has a unique flavor that any apple fancier can detect at once in a pie or in applesauce, a flavor that though mellow never slips into the blandness of the cooked Delicious It is still being planted in commercial orchards in the Northeast. In New York in 1970 it was seventh on the list of varieties planted between 1965 and 1970 with about 70,000 trees planted. In fruit production, which includes fruit from older trees, it ranked second only to the McIntosh with an average of 150-million pounds of apples for the period of 1968–1972. One might almost call it the Methuselah of American apples.

Other older varieties have disappeared completely. I doubt that one can now find a Russet except in an arboretum of old varieties of apples. Yet the Russet was once one of the commonest varieties. A smaller apple, dull green with russet flaking on its skin, rock hard until midwinter, it was actually a mediocre apple both for eating raw and for cooking. Its virtue lay in its keeping ability. Even in an ordinary farmhouse cellar it was known to have kept the year around, last year's apples still being good when the new crop was ripe on the trees. For this reason it was much exported, particularly to England, though it seems to have had no English origin nor to have been grown there. In the days before refrigeration it was carried in ships wherever apples were carried for export, for it could stand long trips without shriveling or losing whatever flavor it had. With modern storage and with shipping under refrigeration, that quality was no longer important, and the Russet disappeared.

The Red Astrachan is another important apple that has almost disappeared with the demise of the home orchard and the reliance upon commercial plantings. Once again, no farm orchard of my childhood would have been without a Red Astrachan tree. It is a Russian apple, imported first to Sweden, thence to England, and thence before 1835 into the United States by the Massachusetts Horticultural Society from the London Horticultural Society. It is one of the earlier ripening apples known as "harvest apples," and the most important of the group. In central New York State it ripens about the middle of August and sometimes earlier. It has absolutely no keeping ability. Two days after it ripens it begins to deteriorate unless put under refrigeration.

A medium-sized apple with a fiery red skin, and much too tart for eating raw, it vies with the Spitzenburg, the Northern Spy, and the Greening for cooking. Of all apples it makes the best jelly and marmalade. Both in jelly and in applesauce made by cooking with the skin and straining, the red color of the skin comes through as bright pink in the finished product. Its flavor both in pies and in applesauce is as good as one can find. Its total lack of keeping ability makes it a complete loss for the modern commercial markets, but it remains a valuable variety for anybody with a home orchard. It can be kept in refrigeration over the winter, but it must be used immediately when brought into warmth. I know of one home owner who puts a couple of bushels in refrigeration each summer for the joy of having Red Astrachan pie and applesauce early the next spring. Its freshly made applesauce, when canned by open kettle method, will hold its taste for a year without deterioration.

The tree unfortunately is a biennial bearer, but there are two varieties extant, which are completely similar except for the fact that their bearing years alternate with each other, so that with sufficient room one can have a tree of each and have Red Astrachans every summer. At the George Landis Arboretum, where we have three Red Astrachan trees, I noted four years ago an interesting phenomenon. The previous year many apple blossoms had fertilized badly or not at all because of a cold, wet spring. One of the Red Astrachan trees, which should have fruited that year but was deprived by the poor fertilization of its fruiting, fruited heavily the next year, when it should not have fruited. For a year or two after that it seemed undetermined in its schedule. Now it seems to be working back to its original timing, though the reversal is not complete. This does suggest the possibility that with modern fruit control chemicals, if one does not object to using them, the fruiting cycle of a Red Astrachan tree might be shifted one year ahead, or that with continual control the tree might be forced into a sparse annual bearing.

The Red Astrachan was one of the four pioneers among Russian apples in America, the other three being Alexander, Tetofsky, and Duchess of Oldenburg; all were brought in at the same time and by the same route. They are all late summer apples, their season being mid–August through September. All are too tart for eating raw but valuable for cooking. Their fruit is quite perishable. Of the four, Alexander and Tetofsky seem to have disappeared, but Duchess, later disseminated through the Midwest and Northwest, proved superior in hardiness to Baldwin, Rhode Island Greening, and Northern Spy, and, therefore, survived in spite of its poor keeping quality. Its fruit is medium to large. The flesh is tinged with yellow, rather firm, moderately fine, crisp, tender, sprightly subacidic, aromatic, and good to very good for cooking but with too much acidity to be good eaten raw. In European nurseries it has been propagated under the names of Char-lamowsky and Botowitsky.

Two other Russian varieties, which entered the United States by different routes, proved valuable and have persisted. One is the Gravenstein, which came by way of Germany, proved at once quite popular in New England, where it is still being grown, and has moved as far south as Delaware and as far west as Oregon and California. Actually, it is almost a duplicate of the Red Astrachan, though it ripens a month later, and probably was a sibling of the Red Astrachan. I do not know the Gravenstein from experience, but that it is a much loved apple in New England, I can testify, for in an article on the older varieties I neglected to discuss it, for the simple reason that I did not know it, and was promptly reprimanded for my omission by many letters from New England apple lovers. That it has the same excellent cooking qualities as the Red Astrachan is evidenced by the report of the manager of a Boston chain of restaurants. During the period when the restaurants were able to use Gravenstein apples for cooking, their daily average sales of apple pie were double that of the average sales for the rest of the year. On the other side of the continent it has become an important commercial variety, particularly in northern California. It actually arrived in California early, for it was planted about 1820 at a Russian settlement near the present Bodega in Sonoma County. Later, in 1863 one William J. Hunt brought budded Gravenstein trees from the East, and from these developed the present concentration of Gravenstein orchards in the vicinity of Sebas-topol.

Another valuable Russian apple is the Yellow Transparent, the earliest of all the harvest apples, which begins to ripen in New York by the Fourth of July. The Yellow Transparent was imported directly from Russia by the USDA in 1870. It is a medium-sized butter yellow apple, juicy and pleasant to the taste, but quickly becomes mushy and dry. For cooking it makes a good applesauce but holds no form. The tree, how-ever, is an annual and heavy bearer, and this combined with its early ripening date has kept it in the trade. It is still available at many fruit nurseries.

A better variety in our area was a slightly larger and whiter apple known locally as the White Transparent. I have been unable to trace this unless it is the variety called Early Harvest in Beach's *Apples of New York*. If so, it was an American apple and was in 1903 already over one-hundred years old. Since I have never heard mention of such an apple in other localities, I suspect that it may have been a chance seedling of the Yellow Transparent, perhaps originating near Oneonta, Otsego County, New York, for all of our local trees seem to have been brought in from the Oneonta area, where it is still quite common and known only as the Transparent. Its fruit keeps no better than the Yellow Transparent, but it is a better cooking apple. A very light yellow applesauce made from the peeled fruit vies for excellence of flavor with the strained applesauce of the Red Astrachan. The tree unfortunately is completely a biennial bearer.

Another group of Russian apples was introduced into Iowa. In 1878 Professor J. L. Budd, head of the Horticultural Department of the Iowa Agricultural College at Ames, imported scions of two hundred varieties of apples from Moscow. Winter hardiness is an apple problem in Iowa, and Budd thought the Russian varieties might solve it. Budd was also secretary for years of the Iowa State Horticultural Society and responsible for its programs. His enthusiasm for the Russian apples he introduced finally almost split the society wide open, for none of the introduced varieties proved successful. Apples that matured just before freezing weather in Russia ripened in July or August in Iowa and would not keep into the winter. They did, however, prove winter hardy, and this quality was used in breeding programs to develop better varieties hardy in Iowa winters.

Another harvest apple, the Sweet Bough, belongs also to a group of apples known as "sweet apples." The sweet apples are, as their name implies, without tartness, and although many of them are delightful eaten raw, they are valueless for applesauce and pies unless they are reinforced with lemon juice. They can be cooked, however, by quartering, coring, and then boiling them with sugar, either with or without their skins, for an hour or two over a low flame. Cooked so, they make a fine sweet dessert.

I have not seen a Sweet Bough for years, but it is still listed occasionally in nursery catalogs. It was, as I remember it, a good-sized green apple with a golden tint, and probably its main distinction is in being a sweet apple that ripens so early. It is an American variety, having arrived on the scene before 1817.

Two other sweet apples used to be common. The Pound Sweet, listed officially as the Pumpkin Sweet, vies among apples for size with the Tompkins King. It is a good eating apple, but it has the unfortunate habit of waterlogging. The flesh of the sections around the core, and sometimes of almost the whole apple, is transformed into a translucent golden green. The transformation, however, does not change the taste.

The other common sweet apple was the Talman Sweet, which was a small butter yellow apple with faint russet dots. Being small, it was used not only for boiling but also for pickling. Since the tree is very hardy, it was at one time used extensively for grafting stock.

The Tompkins King, though not a sweet apple, is the largest apple I have ever seen, specimens often being as big around as the largest grapefruit. It is a showy apple; its skin is red with sunlight yellow shining through. Eaten raw, it has a pleasant tart taste, but cooked, it is not in a class with the Northern Spy. As a tree it was considered desirable because its limbs grew out horizontally and needed little pruning. Also, it is a good annual bearer. It originated as a seedling in northern New Jersey, but a graft was given to one Jacob Mycoff of Tompkins County, New York, who gave it the name of King.

The number of varieties that have been given names runs to over six thousand. During the 1800s, the century of most apple diversity, practically all lists of "best varieties" ran to over a hundred. Out of this diversity the rise and fall of certain varieties is curious and sometimes dramatic. The meteoric ascent and descent of two varieties have all the elements of a stage tragedy. Take for instance the Newtown Pippin. It was the first American apple to attract attention in Europe. When Benjamin Franklin was in London in 1759, he received some specimens, which were much admired. Later, John Bartram sent grafts to Collinson. By 1768 it had come under cultivation in England. By 1773 it was much grown throughout the apple districts of the Atlantic slope, and great quantities were already being exported to England. In that same year Jefferson recorded receiving grafts of the variety, and in 1778 the grafted trees were planted at Monticello. Since the trees grown in England did not ripen their fruit well, export from the colonies to England continued heavily.

The original seedling of Newtown Pippin stood near a swamp on the estate of Gershom Moore in Newtown, Long Island, until 1805, when it died from exhaustion from the cutting of too many scions for grafting, the price of popularity.

In Downing's *The Fruits and Fruit Trees of America*, published in 1856, the Newtown Pippin is credited with "standing at the head of all apples, acknowledged to be unrivaled in all the qualities which constitute a highly flavored dessert apple, commanding the highest price even in Covent Garden Market, London." It was then described as a medium-sized round apple with a green form and a yellow form, perhaps sister seedlings, perhaps one a parent or a branch sport of the other. Both forms attained their best flavor when kept in the cellar until the following March. Like the Russet, its keeping quality was its greatest asset and that which made it such a favorite in London. With the development of refrigeration the importance of keeping quality declined, and the Newtown Pippin began to be ignored. In 1904 it was still being grown in the lower Hudson Valley and the Piedmont and mountain regions of Virginia and North Carolina, but now in the East it has practically disappeared. I have never seen a tree of it nor tasted its fruit. Perhaps I am missing something, like my future citizen brother, who may never know the taste of a Northern Spy.

The strain of the Newtown Pippen, however, is far from extinct. About the turn of the century the yellow form was introduced into the far west under the name of Yellow Newtown. It became particularly successful in the Hood River Valley of Oregon, where its firm flesh and its fine keeping quality still make it a local favorite. To a lesser extent it proved successful in California. Its production in these two regions made it account for 3.1 percent of the total U.S. commercial apple production from 1966–1969. Since I lived in California for several years, I may have tasted a Newtown Pippin after all. I can only say that having grown up on New York Northern Spies and Spitzenburgs, I thought all California apples were tasteless, so if I did eat a Newtown Pippin, I thought it inferior, but the difference in climate may have caused this, not the Newtown Pippin strain itself.

A variety whose ascent and descent were more spectacular was the Baldwin. The Baldwin was a chance seedling on the farm of John Ball, near Lowell, Massachusetts around 1740. For about forty years it was confined to that region, and then its fame began to spread. By the middle of the 1800s it had become the most popular apple in New England, much grown and much exported. In 1904 it was the most important commercial apple in New York State, New England, southern Canada, the southern peninsula of Michigan, and northern Ohio.

Now, there is good reason for the popularity of the Baldwin. It seems to have come from the same strain as the Esopus Spitzenburg, and though its flavor raw is not quite so distinctive nor its tartness for cooking quite equal to the Spitzenburg, it nevertheless has most of the qualities of a good all-purpose apple. It is a larger apple than the Spitzenburg, from a tree easier to grow, and as a keeper it was sufficiently good that it was used for export trade before refrigeration along with the Russet and the Newtown Pippin.

What happened, then? The push of a newcomer, the McIntosh.

The McIntosh came from a strain, the Fameuse, that had dawdled for two hundred years without much success. The

Fameuse, more commonly known in the United States as the Snow because of the glistening whiteness of its flesh, was by most accounts a French apple, of which either a plant or seed was brought to the United States or to southern Quebec from France in the late 1600s. The Snow is a very small apple with a tough but bright red skin. Its white flesh is filled with juice, delicious to eat raw, but too small and too mushy to be desirable for cooking. It was sparingly planted in home orchards. Then, sometime before 1870 the strain yielded a chance seedling on the McIntosh homestead in Dundas County, Ontario, and that chance seedling, the McIntosh, was destined to change the commercial production of all the northeastern United States, even of the whole world.

Some modern hybridizers have guessed that the McIntosh may not have been a seedling of the Snow but of some other related apple of the Fameuse strain. Their reason is that all recent attempts to use the Snow as a parent have produced only inferior progeny. One possibility is that it was a seedling of an apple called Fall St. Lawrence, itself a seedling of the Snow. A possibility for the other parent of the McIntosh may be a Russian apple called the Alexander. If so, the fine eating quality of the McIntosh is one of those surprises that one can always expect in the genus *Malus*.

The popularity of the McIntosh grew slowly at first and then with a rush. In my childhood there was not a single McIntosh tree in the Schoharie Valley of New York, then a high producing apple section. It was, I think, about 1915 that the McIntosh apple began to appear in city markets, and once there it became the apple that everybody wanted. Part of its immediate success may have been its novelty with the public, which had not known so beautiful a red apple, one so tender and with so much juice, so good to the taste. It had, and has, its liabilities. In spite of being an apple beautiful to look at and delicious to bite into, its skin is annoyingly tough. It keeps poorly and when cooked, goes completely to mush, although good tasting mush. Since it ripens early in the season, it quickly superseded Russian varieties like the Gravenstein and the Duchess. It practically wiped the Baldwin out of existence.

In this it was further helped in the Northeast by the severe winter of 1933–1934, which destroyed many old orchards in the area. The McIntosh stock, being hardier than the Baldwin, survived when the Baldwin was killed.

The McIntosh is primarily a cold-country apple. Farther south than Michigan or New York, it becomes an early fall apple, is softer, has a poorer color, and is apt to drop before it is ripe. In the North it has managed to hold its own all during the middle of the century. Even in 1970 its production in New York State led equally with the Rhode Island Greening with an average of 150 million pounds of fruit a year. It was at that time still being planted in commercial orchards at the rate of 150,000 trees a year, but it will have to fight for its place in the future. The danger signals are out for it.

For a while its place was being superseded on the supermarket shelves by an apple of the same strain, the Cortland, unfortunately a cross with a very mediocre variety, the Ben Davis. The Cortland is a larger apple; it keeps and ships better than the McIntosh, but it has lost the sharp edge of taste, which kept the Fameuse strain alive those two hundred years. Many hybrids have been made with the McIntosh as a parent in the United States, in Canada, and in England, but except for the hardiness of the ones developed in Canada, none seem sufficiently valuable to replace the McIntosh. One hybrid of McIntosh with Jersey Black, made by the Agricultural Experiment Station at Geneva, New York, and called the Macoun, dawdled with little interest for fifty years but in the last decade shows signs of becoming popular for the simple reason that its taste is superior. This is a good sign for the apples of the future. It is perhaps the first time in the last fifty years that taste rather than profit to commercial orchardists has brought an apple into popularity. However, this one hopeful sign is far counterbalanced by the fact that the long supremacy of the McIntosh is really being threatened, not by any of its progeny, but by the Delicious and the Golden Delicious, neither of which approach the McIntosh in taste or in all-around usability.

This emergence of inferior varieties to rule the roost is discussed later, but with the trend must be related the emergence in the mid-1900s of an older variety, the Rome Beauty. This originated in 1816 as a chance sprout from a grafting rootstock on the farm of Joel Gillett at Proctorville, Ohio. After the usual local interest in a new variety, it was singled out by the Ohio Convention of Fruit Growers in 1848 and began to be planted in the Midwest. It was not until the second decade of the 1900s that it began to attain national importance. Beach in 1904 reported that it was little known among New York fruit growers. Yet by 1970 it was third in New York production and fourth in new plantings. In the decades 1950– 1970 it has been one of the common varieties on the supermarket shelves. The reason for its rise is the transference of apple production from the home orchard to the commercial orchard. Rome Beauty is a good money-maker. It has a nice red color; it keeps and bears handling exceptionally well; and its regular-shaped fruit make it well adapted for commercial processing. Nobody seems to worry much about the fact that it is an inferior-tasting apple, either eaten raw or cooked.

Another old variety that has had an erratic history is the York Imperial. Its beginning is interesting. It was a wild seedling on the farm of a Mr. Johnson, near York, Pennsylvania, in the early years of the 1800s. Johnson paid no attention until he noticed that the school children were visiting it in early spring to eat the apples that had been preserved under the snow. He tried the apples himself, found they were still excellent eating, and induced a local nurseryman to propagate from the tree under the name of Johnson's Fine Winter. The nurseryman found little market for the stock and dumped most of it into a hollow beside the turnpike passing his place. The thrifty Pennsylvania farmers going past picked up the free offering and planted them on their farms, and to this it owes its first distribution. In the middle of the century it was called to the attention of the horticulturist Charles Downing, who called it the "imperial of keepers" and suggested the name of York Imperial. Its extraordinary keeping quality appealed to the commercial growers of the Pennsylvania– Virginia area, and it soon became widely planted. By the 1880s it had spread over into Ohio and the Midwest. During the early 1900s, it was widely grown in the Appalachian region and along with Baldwin found a ready market for exporting to Europe, particularly to England. By 1930 electric refrigeration had been introduced, and the keeping quality of York Imperial was not so important. Also about that time England began to place sharp restrictions upon the import of apples. With the loss of a good export market, York Imperial was about to follow the eclipse of the Baldwin, but just at that time two of its hitherto unnoticed qualities saved it from oblivion. During World War II, the commercial processing of apples gained importance. Now, commercial processors like an apple with a yellow flesh, for this gives an attractive color both to applesauce and the slices for pie. York Imperial has the desired yellow flesh, and what proved equally important to the processors, it has a very small core, which means less waste in the processing. So the processing of York Imperial, which started as a salvaging of unsalable fruit, became a commercial success, and York Imperial began to be planted again. It has become once more one of the important varieties in the Appalachian region.

One variety that gained importance when it was transferred to another climate is the Bellflower. It was formerly fairly common in home orchards in the Northeast, where it often went under the name of White Spitzenburg, but it never attained commercial importance there. It may have had an origin from French seed, since the name was sometimes given as Bellefleur, but the original tree, large and old, was in 1817 still standing on a farm in Burlington County, New Jersey. The tree is large and vigorous. The fruit, lemon to butter yellow, sometimes with a pink cheek, ripens late in October but even then is not at its best. It is one of the better keepers of the old apples, but it has the added advantage that its flavor improves during the keeping, and it is at its very best for eating raw when it has been stored in a cellar until March or April of the next spring. It is then a delicious apple with a mellow taste equal in quality to the taste of a cooked Greening. Neither taste, as far as my experience goes, has ever been duplicated in other apples. For cooking it is not quite tart enough to rate with the Greening. It was introduced rather early into the

Midwest, but there too it became only moderately popular. In the late 1800s it found in the coastal sections of California a climate that seemed perfectly adapted to its best growth, and there during the early 1900s it was the leading commercial variety. Now, its reign there is yielding to the Golden Delicious, not a better apple, but commercially more profitable.

Another variety from New Jersey, the Winesap, proved to be more successful in the Piedmont section of Virginia. In the more northern apple sections the tree proved short-lived and the fruit small, but in the Midwest and the Far West it grew well and became one of the most popular commercial varieties during the late 1800s. It is a brilliant red apple, excellent for eating raw or for cooking, but its outstanding quality again was its keeping ability. It fact, it keeps so well that even today where it is still grown it is kept in ordinary storage and not in the more modern air controlled refrigeration. Its popularity has been eroded by its tendency to small size and competition from other varieties that can be kept by air controlled storage for the next spring and early summer market. This is a pity, for it is a far better apple than the varieties that are taking its place, such as the Delicious.

Most apple varieties, however, succeed best in the section of the country where they originate and often are failures when planted in a different climate. Each variety, in general, has its own particular requirements of length of season, amount of rainfall, and amount of heat needed for its best development. I have already mentioned the failure of the Russian apples when tried in Iowa. The Baldwin becomes a fall apple in Virginia and Arkansas and loses the edge of its taste.

A variety that best illustrates the danger of transfer to another climate is the Ben Davis. Its origin is unknown, though definitely in the South before 1800. Kentucky, Tennessee, and Virginia all have claimed it. By the time of the Civil War, it had got to Missouri and during 1875 to 1900 was disseminated throughout all the apple-growing portions of the United States. Even at its best in the South it was a mediocre apple, but it did produce well in warm climates, was a brilliant red—oh, that bright color that has so often raised a mediocre apple to prominence—and was a good keeper. Its success in the South prompted some commercial orchards in the Northeast to plant it, but the results were catastrophic to the growers. It did not ripen well in the North, and it had to compete with varieties like the Northern Spy and the Greening. Orchardists planted good stands of it and brought them to production, only to find that buyers bought the fruit one year and never again. There was nothing to do but tear the trees out and replace them with a variety whose flesh was not dry, coarse, and tasteless.

I said that the taste of a Bellflower eaten raw the next April or of a Rhode Island Greening cooked has never been duplicated, but I speak actually from little knowledge. Of the thousands of varieties that have been grown in the United States, I know only a few. In 1845 the catalog of the Prince Nursery on Long Island offered 350 varieties of apples, including the Baldwin—three hundred and fifty varieties. Think of the different tastes one will never know, the fascinating names of apples never to be tasted: the Fallawater, whose only claim to distinction seems to have been its size; the Blue Pearmain, one of a whole group of Pearmains; and the Black Gilliflower, a long red apple with a pointed nose. Perhaps the Black Gilliflower is the apple I knew as the Sheep's Nose, though our Sheep's Nose was more green than red with dull reddish streaks and a solid, somewhat mealy flesh. It was perhaps one of the ancestors of the Delicious, for it was as dry to the lips and as insipid to the tongue, its only distinction being its strange shape.

Of interest too, and often amusing, is the way certain apples got their names, and the number of names for the same apple. The Bottle Greening, which originated on the border of New York and Vermont, got its name from the fact that the original old tree was hollow, and workmen in the vicinity used to store their bottles of hard cider in it during the daytime to keep them cool. The Smokehouse was named from the original tree that grew near a smokehouse, the tiny wooden building, usually looking like a misplaced privy, where hams were smoked, on the farm of William Gibbons, Lancaster County, Pennsylvania. This was in the early 1800s, and the Smokehouse is still a favorite apple in the Pennsylvania Dutch section but never seems to have been good enough to extend its range.

In reading over descriptions of old varieties, one wonders too over the highly touted varieties that never made good: the Boiken, for instance, a German apple that came well recommended; the Buckingham, a southern apple important enough to collect synonyms like the Fall Queen of Kentucky, Bachelor, and Winter Queen (Was this modern, sexual trend prefigured?); and the Kittigeskee, which originated with the Cherokee Indians in western North Carolina, was sent to France in 1860, and proved popular there, but is now forgotten here.

On the other hand there are many varieties that proved popular in a small way and still hold a small popularity over a large area: the Swaar, a deep yellow apple, of which Downing wrote, "This is a truly noble American fruit produced by the Dutch settlers on the Hudson, near Esopus," and which is still grown in some sections; the Grimes Golden, one of the best known yellow apples before the Golden Delicious replaced it; the Wealthy, a hardy northern apple still grown in Minnesota; the Hubbardston, originating in Hubbardston, Massachusetts, before 1832 and once a leading commercial variety in New England and New York, though never more than a mediocre apple; and the Lady Apple, a small French apple over three hundred years old, called the Api in France, which still persists in some localities for the fancy Christmas trade. It makes the mouth water to think of them all.

The sad fact is that we have let the gene pool grow limited. Intensive breeding primarily for commercial purposes and the disappearance of small farm orchards have already limited the possibilities of future development. Unless the apple is going to become a standardized mediocre fruit, the main emphasis in the immediate future should be on taste. What we need now are apples that will bear annually, keep well, ship well, look beautiful in a supermarket bin, and at the same time taste as good as a Northern Spy or a Spitzenburg. If we cannot do that, then we have failed. Judging by the signs of the varieties popular at the moment, we are failing.

4. O Beautiful Red Sawdust

The present picture of the eating apple in the United States and, perhaps in the world, cannot be viewed without apprehension. Production and the market begin to be dominated by two varieties, the Delicious and the Golden Delicious, both inferior varities when judged by the standard set by the Northern Spy. Why? The answer is simple. Apple production has become big business, and both the Delicious and the Golden Delicious are good money-makers for commercial orchardists over a wide spread of country. The trees bear heavily and with proper care, annually. Both varieties seem able to adapt themselves to a great variety of climates and soils without much change in the quality of their fruit. The fruit of both is attractive, does not bruise easily when handled, ships well, and keeps exceptionally well both under ordinary and controlled storage, and last but not least, both varieties have had superb publicity.

Since this century might almost be characterized in the United States as the Madison Avenue Age, it is not surprising that the current top favorites owe much of their success to good advertising. Up to about 1920 an apple arrived at top production largely because of two features, its ability to keep well and to taste good both raw and cooked. Whatever promotion it got was mostly accidental. It is doubtful if either of the current favorites could have attained their present position without a good deal of pushing.

It is typical too that accounts of the origin of each are surrounded by partially embellished melodrama, as opposed to the casual and factual history of the older varieties. The Delicious, for instance, has a monument erected to it in Hope, Iowa. Nothing could better illustrate the genius of our age for crowning mediocrity, unless it be some of the elected presidents of the period.

Stripped of all their melodramatic embellishments, the various stories of the origin of the Delicious agree on all of their basic facts except one. What seems sure is that it was a chance tree in the orchard of one Jesse Hiatt near Peru in Madison County, Iowa. Hiatt was a middle-aged Quaker farmer and amateur apple breeder with two varieties already to his credit,

Hiatt Sweet and Hiatt Black, which he sold locally. Right here at the beginning are two versions that vary. One says the he set out a grafted Bellflower, that the graft died, but that the root sent up a shoot so vigorous that it was saved. The other version says that the tree was a chance seedling growing outside of the regular rows, near an old Bellflower tree, and was saved because of its vigor. Whatever its origin, the tree bore its first fruit when it was ten years old. Mr. Hiatt thought the fruit superior, named it the Hawkeye, and in subsequent years sent samples of the fruit to various Iowa fairs, where it was ignored. He also tried to induce his friend, Judge W. H. Lewis, a nurseryman, to graft and sell the trees, but Lewis saw no future in the apple. A story goes that Hiatt in peddling his apples once met on the road a Mr. Gorshorn, publisher of the local newspaper and a large orchardist. Hiatt presented Gorshorn with one of his Hawkeye apples and tried to interest him in propagating and selling the variety. Gorshorn later told his son that old man Hiatt was batty and his apple, no good. These stories are usually told to emphasize how unobservant were these early tasters of the Delicious. To a New Yorker raised on the Northern Spy and the Spitzenburg, the commonplace thought is that from the point of view of an excellent household apple, men like Gorshorn and Lewis knew what they were talking about.

Nevertheless, Hiatt persisted and found his success, if not his personal reward. Now, real promotion enters the picture. In 1893 Hiatt sent four of his Hawkeye apples to the Stark Brothers Nurseries in Louisiana, Missouri, who sponsored each year a Stark Fruit Fair for which they sought fruits from all over the world. According to one account, when C. M. Stark, then president of Stark Brothers Nurseries, bit into one of the Hawkeyes, he exclaimed, "My, that's delicious—and that will be its name." Another account says that he had been for several years carrying a jotting of the name Delicious in one of his little notebooks, waiting for an apple to which he might apply it. Whatever the truth of this is, the amusing fact is that although the apple was given the prize in that year's fair, the name of the sender was lost. Next year, however, Mr.

Hiatt sent a barrel of his Hawkeyes to the Stark Fruit Fair, and with this Stark Brothers Nurseries and Orchard Company, as the firm was then officially called, took over the promotion of the new variety under the name of Delicious. It is said that Stark Brothers spent over three-quarters of a million dollars to introduce and popularize the new variety, and this at the turn of the century was a lot of money. No one can say now that financially it was not a good investment.

From the very beginning on superlative after superlative was piled upon the variety. Mr. Stark claimed it was the most delicious apple he had ever eaten.Mr. Hiatt said, "All declare it to be the best apple in the world. Once it is introduced, there will be little call for the Jonathan." Later A. J. Mason, former president of the Hood River Oregon Apple Growers' Union, said, "It is the best-flavored apple I have ever tasted," and W. P. Powell of *The Orchard and Fruit Garden* hailed it as the "noblest apple of the world today."

This is a good time for a pause of consideration. To one who has tasted a good Northern Spy, this praise of the Delicious is ridiculous. What is the basis of judgment? What caused it?

I think the answer must be primarily color. Although Hiatt's Hawkeye was actually a striped red apple, sporting strains soon developed the clear red apple that we know today. As such, it is perhaps the most beautiful apple ever developed in the United States, that large well-shaped apple with the fiery red skin that will take a polish like the hood of the latest hard top out of Detroit. One could write an essay upon the fascination for the American public of the color red upon a fruit. That the skin is thick and tough and almost inedible seems to have counted for nothing. This is the apple's preservative, this and the solid flesh which will make an apple stand up maybe for weeks on the fruit stand run by the woman on the corner, never shriveling, always returning after the morning's wipe to the same shining red cone, still salable after days of exposure, though to the teeth and tongue penetrating into it, it may be like slightly flavored sawdust: the Delicious, the Delicious.

One can discount the statements of all the promoters. Madison Avenue always exaggerates. One can also suggest that in the areas in which the Delicious has received most promotion, it may seem superior because better-tasting apples do not grow well or do not keep their edge of flavor in those climates. In general, the apples with an edge to their flavor come mostly from the colder regions of apple bearing. Neither Missouri nor the State of Washington are such areas. One might wonder if the average man of those areas knows what a superior apple tastes like, but this argument does not hold up well, because both in Iowa, where Jesse Hiatt lived, and in Washington the Jonathan was and still is a well-known apple, and the Jonathan, although small, really is a superior apple.

To get back to the fundamentals of the origin of the Delicious, let's examine the facts. If the account which says that the original tree was a grafted Bellflower, of which the grafted top died and only the stock produced a tree, then its origin could be anything that either a nursery or Hiatt himself might have used for grafting stock, unless one counts the very unlikely chance of a graft influencing the stock, a not completely unknown, but very rare occurrence. If the other account, which makes it a chance seedling near an old Bellflower tree is correct, then the Bellflower is most likely one of its parents. The large size and shape of the fruit might agree. It is a little hard to believe, however, that a one-generation cross of the bright yellow Bellflower would produce such a dramatic change in color, although it is not impossible. Here, however, it must be considered that the original Hawkeye of Hiatt was a streaked red apple. There is still the loss of taste to account for.

I have always wondered if the old Black Gilliflower might not be in the ancestry. The Black Gilliflower has the same color, the same tough skin, the same shape, the same texture of flesh, and the same lack of taste. The Bellflower, on the other hand, is a very tasty apple. I have tried to find out if the Black Gilliflower was much or ever grown in Iowa but so far without any sure answer. Records are scant, but it may be indicative that Hiatt had named one of his previous hybrids the Hiatt Black, which sounds like a dark red apple and may suggest that he had a Black Gilliflower in his orchard.

Compared to some of the older varieties, the rise to fame of the Delicious was more rapid. Taken over by the Stark Brothers Nurseries in 1894, it had by 1920 become a prominent apple in many sections of the country, not in the Northeast where the McIntosh was the vigorous newcomer, but in the plains states and particularly in the Northwest, for it quicky became apparent that the Delicious was a variety most suited to the climate and soil of Oregon and Washington. It was perhaps the beauty of the fruit of the Delicious raised in those two states that clinched its success. The northwestern fruit growers were quick to realize that they had a gold mine on their hands. Since it was a beautiful red apple that was so much in demand, there began a frantic search to develop a strain of Delicious that would be bigger, redder, and more productive than ever.

Actually, a sport of the original Delicious planted in New Jersey led the way to the later development. The liability of the original Delicious had been that it did not develop its superior red color until late, so that fruit picked when the color was good was apt to have lost its crispness. In 1921 a tree in the orchard of Lewis Mood in Monroeville, New Jersey, developed a sporting branch which produced fruit that colored early. The Stark Brothers Nurseries purchased the tree, propagated from the sporting branch, and named the new variety the Starking.

This appearance of a sporting branch on a Delicious tree was the first evidence of an ability of the Delicious variety to sport that was to lead eventually to an orgy of selection of slight mutations, sometimes of a whole tree, more often of a fruiting branch. Its genetic makeup is obviously unstable. Except for the 1921 selection, only a few early notices were taken of sports, but during the 1940s the success of the Delicious strain in the Northwest led to more careful observation of branch mutation, and during the fifties and sixties every orchardist and nurseryman was on the watch for a branch with better production, larger fruit, and brighter color. By 1969 the situation had become so absurd that the Cooperative Extension Service of the College of Agriculture of Washington State

University issued a bulletin listing the various selected strains of the Delicious apple and trying somewhat to evaluate them. There are over 130 strains in the list.

The genus *Malus* was showing no signs of losing its genetic fertility and variability.

In the meantime the Delicious has risen to lead all other varieties of apples in production in the United States. It has made the apple industry of the Northwest famous. It has probably made more money for orchardists than any other variety in United States history. For the commercial orchardist then it is the goose that laid the golden egg. It has almost all the qualities they could desire: a vigorous tree that produces abundantly and, if on fertile soil, annually, and large fruit that is attractive in color and that keeps exceptionally well. Unfortunately for the apple connoisseur, it lacks only one thing: taste.

The Golden Delicious, which at the moment is the only variety that threatens the commercial supremacy of the Delicious, has no genetic relation at all to the Delicious. Its name was given it merely to capitalize upon the success of the Delicious, and its success follows somewhat the same course as that of the Delicious. Its ancestry is guessed to be a cross between a European variety called Golden Reinette, a small yellow dessert apple long known and esteemed in England, and a variety called Grimes Golden, which itself seems to have been a spontaneous seedling in West Virginia sometime before 1804. The guess is that the male pollen from Golden Reinette fertilized a Grimes Golden ovary. What is known is that around 1800 one Bewell Mullins, who ran a thirty-six-acre farm in Clay County, West Virginia, or perhaps his father, bought a few Golden Reinette trees from an itinerant peddler and planted them along the pasture fence in back of the farmhouse. In time the trees matured, and from the scattered excess fruit a young orchard gradually grew up. In the meantime Bewell Mullins, wanting a larger farm for his three sons, had traded the farm to his uncle, Anderson H. Mullins, for Anderson's larger farm. Anderson was a great fruit enthusiast, and he was quick to notice the unusual fruit of one of the seedlings. It seemed superior to all of the other yellow-fruited trees in the area, producing more and larger fruit with exceptional keeping quality. For a few years he sold the fruit locally, and it became known as Mullins' Yellow Seedling. In April of 1914 Anderson decided to try for greater success. he sent three apples from the tree to Stark Brothers Nurseries, describing not only its fine size and color, but remarking particularly upon its keeping quality—the apples keeping in good condition in his dirt-floor cellar until late spring—and upon the fact that the tree bore heavily even on years when other trees fruited poorly.

The apples and Anderson's account sufficiently interested Paul Stark, then President of Stark Brothers Nurseries, to make him journey to West Virginia the next autumn to have a look at the tree. Convinced of its worth, he bought it for five-thousand dollars. Here one slight ambiguity enters the story. Anderson Mullins fades out of the picture, and Bewell Mullins appears again. Perhaps the property still belonged to Bewell. At any rate, all subsequent dealings with Stark Brothers Nurseries were with Bewell Mullins. Paul Stark had a wire cage erected around the tree to preserve it from marauders and paid Bewell one hundred dollars a year to take care of it. Then he went home, and being Madison Avenue minded, proceeded to his publicity. Presumably it was the growing success of the Delicious that made him change the name Mullins' Yellow Seedling to Golden Delicious, for the only resemblance or relation of the new apple to the Delicious was its elongated shape with slightly flattened ends. Even this is a curious fact in the history of apple variety success, for one of the reasons that Hiatt's Hawkeye had had slow going at the beginning was its shape. People were accustomed then to round apples; a long pointed apple was a freak. Now the tables were turned. A long pointed apple was fashionable.

There is no doubt that Paul Stark laid his publicity well. His firm propagated the apple heavily and advertised it heavily. He aroused the interest of the American Fruit Growers. He managed to get a Wilder Silver Medal for it from the American Pomological Society. He even managed to get Queen Marie of

Roumania to eat one publicly during her tour of the United States. Today, it is undoubtedly the up-and-coming favorite.

Again, why?

Probably for much the same reasons as the rise of the Delicious. It is a valuable commercial apple, growing well, bearing early, and producing abundantly over a large geographic range. It has spread to Tasmania, South Africa, and Mexico. In all these localities it continues to grow well, bear well, and keep well, and it is now yielding good so-called "spur" sports with short stiff branchlets, which bear fruit earlier and even more heavily.

Now the Golden Delicious is by no means as inferior an apple as the Delicious. At its best it can be a very delicious apple to eat raw, but in this it is variable, both from season to season and from locality to locality. For cooking it is simply too bland to be of more than mediocre value. Sharpened with lemon juice it can make a good apple pie, but the taste is no longer pure apple. Compared, therefore, to an all purpose apple like the Northern Spy or the McIntosh, or even the Baldwin, it is outclassed.

But it is here to stay a while, no doubt about that. It is too good a money-maker to be discarded lightly. Perhaps it may perform one valuable function. It may awaken the American public to the fact that an apple does not have to be bright shining red to be good to eat.

5. Chemical Nightmare

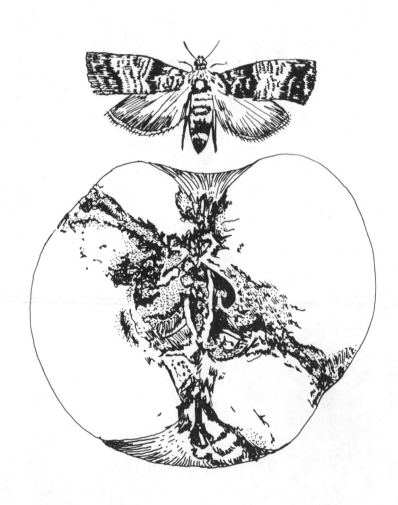

Having now sketched the ancestry of a few of the common and uncommon apples, I will try to trace the more intimate and short-term history of one individual apple, your "apple a day to keep the doctor away."

Let us assume that you live in a large city and have to buy your apples from a supermarket or a specialty fruit store, and let us consider the apple that you eat on a certain March day, toward the end of winter. Let us assume that you were lucky in your buying and are eating a McIntosh apple, juicy and rich in taste, one of the good varieties still sold in supermarkets.

Unless your McIntosh came from a super, super specialty fruit store that ordered its apples from some small orchard in Vermont or Ontario, your apple would have come from a commercial apple orchard. On the same March day of the year before, your McIntosh apple would have been a tight but fat round flower bud on a McIntosh tree, one tree out of fifty or a hundred or a thousand, depending upon the size of the commercial orchard. About the time that your flower bud was just beginning to swell, the orchard would have been sprayed with a soil fumigant named dieldrin which contains not less than eighty-five percent of 1,2,3,4,10,10-hexachloro-6, 7-epoxy-1, 4, 4a, 5, 6, 7, 8, 8a-octahydro-1, 4-endo-exo-5, 8-dimethanonaphthalene and not less than fifteen percent active related compounds. To the dieldrin spray would have been added some organophosphate compound, and the two together would have served to protect the soil and the trees against cutworms, lygus bugs, stink bugs, San Jose scale, and certain destructive mites. At the stage of bud opening, called the pre-pink stage, when the leaves were just unfolding but the flower bud was still tight, the orchard would have been sprayed with parathion (0,0-diethyl 0-para-nitrophenyl phosphorothioate), one of the most toxic of all organic pesticides against tent caterpillars, leaf rollers, assorted bugs, and also with some fungicide, such as lime sulphur, or more likely an organic fungicide such as dodine (N-dodecylguanidine acetate) against apple scab and apple mildew. When the flower bud was fully open, the orchard would have been sprayed with Elgetol (sodium salt of 2,methyl-4,0-dinitrophenol), a chemical that causes the tree to abort some of its flowering ovaries and, therefore, to limit the fruit set. Possibly this spraying would have been delayed until the flower petals were shed, and then Sevin (carbaryl: 1-naphthyl-N-methylcarbamate) used in place of Elgetol. Two weeks later the orchard would have been sprayed with Guthion (0, 0 - dimethyl S - [4-oxo-1, 2, 3-benzotriazin-3 (4H) -ylmethyl] phosphorodithioate) against codlin moth and perhaps with captan (N-trichloromethylthio-4-cyclohexene 1,2-dicarboximide) against bull's-eye rot. About three weeks later it would have received another spraying of Guthion, plus Thiodan (6,7,8,9,10,10- hexachloro - 1,5,5a,6,9,9a - hexahydro - 6,9-methano-2,4,3-benzo(e)-dioxathiopin-3-oxide) against the woolly apple aphid.

By now it would be summer with grass and weeds growing high among the trees, and to kill the herbage, the orchard would have been sprayed with 2,4-D (2, 4-dichlorophenoxy-acetic acid). Actually this would be only a secondary herbicide application, the first having been made on the bare ground of either the previous November or of early spring with a spraying of simazine (2-chloro-4, 6-bis(ethylamino)-s-triazine) or paraquat (1,1'-dimethyl-4,4'-bipyridinium salt).

In September, four to fourteen days before the expected harvest, the trees would have been sprayed with Ethrel to promote red color and with NAA (1-naphthaleneacetic acid) to prevent your apple from dropping off the tree before it was ripe.

Now, in early fall your McIntosh apple, being one of the lucky surviving fruits, was picked and rushed into cold storage, or since it was a McIntosh, probably into atmospherically controlled storage.

Controlled atmosphere storage is a method that has been devised for keeping apples in good condition longer than they will keep in ordinary refrigeration. Apples, after tree ripening and picking, carry on a process known as respiration. In the presence of oxygen in the air, the fruit sugars in the apple are gradually oxidized. The flesh of the apple softens, the taste changes, and the color of the skin changes. This change occurs rather rapidly in McIntosh apples kept in ordinary refrigeration. Also, when McIntosh apples are held at extended periods at thirty-two degrees Fahrenheit, the core section of the apple is apt to turn brown.

Under controlled atmosphere storage the fruit is kept at a low temperature in an atmosphere in which the amount of oxygen is lowered and the amount of carbon dioxide, the end product of oxidation, is increased. Under controlled atmosphere storage the refrigeration chamber is sealed, and by controlled ventilation and the removal of excess carbon dioxide, the atmosphere is kept with the desired ratios of oxygen and carbon dioxide.

Unfortunately, not all varieties of apples respond equally well to controlled atmosphere storage. Many in time develop a discoloration known as scald, which makes the fruit unsalable. It has been found, however, that certain chemicals will inhibit the scald. The two effective ones are ethoxyquin and diphenylamine (DPA). Ethoxyquin (6-ethoxy-1, 2-dihydro-2, 2, 4-trimethylquinoline) is most commonly used, and the method of treatment is to dip the apples completely in a solution just before putting them into the controlled atmosphere chamber.

Two weeks before you purchased your apple, it was retrieved from its controlled atmosphere storage vault and rushed to the supermarket with the hope that it would stay firm and not discolored until you bought it.

So there is your apple, almost a chemical apple, and there is the practice in the modern commercial apple orchard. It is, merely in its summary, a frightening history for a fruit. And lest you think that I am exaggerating, the spray program that I have just outlined is taken from the 1974 *Spray Guide for Tree Fruits in Eastern Washington,* published by the Cooperative Extension Service of the College of Agriculture of Washington State University.

At the other side of the United States, the *1975 Tree Fruit Recommendations for Commercial Growers*, issued by the New York State College of Agriculture and Life Sciences at Cornell University, is even more liberal in its use of chemicals. Its soil fumigation program does not include dieldrin, which has been banned in New York State, but it does contain a list of nine others. Also, instead of the rather open period following petal fall in the Washington program, Cornell recommends a spray when three-quarters of the petals have fallen, another seven to ten days after petal fall, called the "first cover spray," another eight to twelve days later called the "second cover spray," another eight to twelve days after that called the "third cover spray," and then adds: "Subsequent cover sprays are spaced at regular intervals or timed for pest control depending upon the situation and the insecticide used."

The states of Washington and New York are the two largest commercial producers of apples in the United States, and the experiment stations that recommend the chemicals for your apple are subsidiaries of two of the most important universities in those states.

Had I been quoting such a summary ten years ago, the spray schedule would have included three or four sprayings of DDT during the summer. DDT (1,1,1-trichloro-2,2-bis (P-chlorophenyl)ethane) has received more notoriety than other chemicals used in pest control, not necessarily because it is the most dangerous but because being cheap to produce, it was used more. It is one of the many organochlorides that unfortunately leave residues in the soil, in animals in the soil, in water, in animals in the water, and in the air. Particularly, its residues are passed on from animal to animal in a predator-prey chain. The residue is insufficient to kill the worms and slugs or the fish that eat plankton in lakes, but it builds up and up in the fatty tissues of their bodies until the amount becomes lethal. This buildup in fatty tissues is almost unbelievable. In the disastrous death of the breeding colonies of western grebes on Lake Clear, California, after three successive applications of DDT in 1949, 1954, and 1957 to kill the larvae of gnats which were annoying fishermen, an analysis of the visceral fat of two dead grebes revealed a concentration of DDT eighty thousand times as great as the concentration of DDT in the lake water. The same sort of buildup occurs in the worm-slug-bird food chains.

Following all this notoriety and the persistent prodding of conservationists and other farseeing persons, but not for the most part prodding by either the state or university experiment stations nor by the USDA experiment stations, with the exception of the Patuxent Wild Life USDA Research Center at Laurel, Maryland, the use of DDT has now been banned in most of the United States, and in most of the large industrial nations of the world.

What about the chemicals which have not been banned, those which are still being recommended for the preservation of your perfect McIntosh apple? Are they dangerous? Yes, many of them are so dangerous that the same bulletin which recommends one of the programs I have outlined devotes its first four pages to warnings, two pages to the hazards to workers who apply the chemicals, and two pages to the hazards of the chemicals, if not properly applied, to desired insects like bees and certain predatory mites that feed upon other mites, or to desired vegetable growth, such as the leaves on the apple trees or crops in the fields next to the orchards.

What is their danger to you who are eating this McIntosh apple? Not much, if you are careful to wash the apple well, because apple trees do not pick up large amounts of chemicals from the soil and transport them to their fruits. Had your apple been a turnip or a beet or a carrot, then you might have been in danger, for the root vegetables do accumulate chemicals. Also, should your apple have been one that was not eaten raw but was used for processing, then there might have been danger, particularly in the end products such as apple juice and vinegar, which are largely made from the peelings and the pomace, since there might have been danger of careless washing of the fruit, plus the fact that whatever residue might have been picked up by a fruit tree tends to be concentrated in the peel or skin of the fruit.

What about the persons who live near the orchard where the apple was grown, the persons who live near the streams which drain that orchard, or even the persons a thousand miles from that orchard? The answer to this is that nobody really knows, that only a few care, and that seemingly—and this is the disgraceful crux of the matter—that few persons in organizations responsible for the use of these chemicals take the danger seriously. I say disgraceful because most of the experiment stations that made the recommendations for the use of these chemicals are adjuncts of colleges and universities. We have thought of our colleges and universities as the intellectual centers of the nation, and one would expect from them a search for the truth underlying all the affairs of life, including dangers to the countryside and to the desirable plants, insects, animals, birds, fish, and men living in it. Certainly, research into this should be conducted at these centers.

The sad fact is that the university and state experiment stations are devoted to searching for ways the commerical apple grower can raise the most fruit with the least possible expense. If the apple that the grower produces is an inferior apple and if the chemicals that the grower uses in its production are a possible menace to the countryside in which the apple is grown and to the drainage area below it, including the drinking water from its underground wells, not much more than lip service is paid to the danger.

It is true that there is voluminous literature on what happens to these chemicals that are now used in cultivation, not only of apples, but of grains, rice, tobacco, and vegetables. A great deal of experimentation has been done, but most of it has been devoted to helping the grower to be a little less of a menace than he has been before, or better said, how to be a menace not great enough to be penalized by law. Yet in many ways these experiment stations control the apple that you are eating, because it is they who advise the prospective owner what varieties of apples are likely to make him the most money. He doesn't, of course, have to follow their advice, but he is apt to follow it. If they tell him to spray the weeds in his orchard with 2,4-D, which is "quickly degradable," he leans back on this glib assurance of moral integrity and sprays with 2,4-D.

The problem of accumulating toxic material in the soil and biota is preeminently a problem of this century, and it results directly from the mass production of agricultural products. Of all agricultural products it is most intense in orchards, because the pests, both insect and fungus, which destroy or disfigure fruit, take the most toxic material to control. When the major production of apples was from small farm orchards scattered throughout the country, the pest problem was not so severe. It is when a one-crop agriculture takes over a section of countryside that the trouble becomes intense.

It was not until about 1890 that growers began to use Bordeaux mixture against apple scab (*Venutria inaequalis*). Bordeaux mixture unfortunately caused russeting of the fruit. In 1909–1910 the Cornell University Agricultural Experiment Station advised the use of lime sulphur, and this and later elemental sulphur replaced the use of Bordeaux. Unfortunately again, the sulphur reduced the ability of the apple leaves in photosynthesis and so reduced the yield of fruit. In 1940 with the advent of the organic chemicals, Fermate replaced the sulphur.

In the meantime, the other particularly destructive pest of apples, the codlin moth (*Carpocapsa pomonella*), had been controlled by arsenic sprays, either lead arsenate, sodium arsenite, or arsenic trioxide. Nobody for a long time paid any attention to the accumulation from these sprays of arsenic in the soil, until it became evident that the residual arsenic in orchard soils was becoming destructive to small vegetation. Even then nobody considered the damage to animals, birds, or men. Land that had been orchard and was later converted to cereal, forage, or vegetable crops proved useless. Nothing would grow well on it. Even young apple trees planted as replacements in orchards long in use died. Then, the bugbear of insect resistance, which was to prove so troublesome later with the chemicals, began. As arsenic came to have less effect, orchardists had no recourse except to use more arsenic. In the Pacific Northwest some areas accumulated residues of arsenic trioxide up to fourteen hundred pounds per acre. Finally, the amount of arsenic on the fruit made it dangerous and unsalable. Great Britain refused to buy American apples.

Then, in 1945 came DDT. The story from then on is better known, but the lesson of it is still not thoroughly learned. In the first euphoria for this all-purpose insecticide, and a cheap one at that, commercial orchardists went wild. Spraying several times during the summer was common. Persons who lived next to apple orchards had to stay away from home during the spraying season. Bluebirds almost disappeared. Robins decreased. These are the feeders on earthworms and grubs, which accumulate DDT without themselves being killed. The accumulation of DDT in the soils of apple orchards was tremendous. In a study of twelve apple orchards, the accumulation of DDT in the soils after six years of DDT spraying ranged from 35 to 113 pounds per acre under the trees, and from 26 to 61 pounds per acre between the trees. Aldrin and dieldrin, sometimes used for insects in the soil as well as on blossoms and fruit, were as bad. Aldrin itself did not persist long, but in the soil it was transformed into the more deadly dieldrin, which did persist. All three of these pesticides have now been banned in many states and in whole nations, but as late as 1974 the Spray Program of Washington State University, which I summarized earlier, still suggested dieldrin for soil fumigation. Next to DDT it is one of the most persistent in the environment of the organochlorides, its half-life being over two years.

In this same year, 1974, the State of Washington restricted the use of forty-three pesticides to commercial growers, commercial applicators, and government agencies, and these were sold only by licensed pesticide dealers. The reason given for this was that the most dangerous pesticides were to be sold only to persons experienced in their use and aware of their hazards. What such restrictions boil down to is that you and I, the little men, cannot use these dangerous things on our little half acre of land but that a commercial fruit grower can saturate his hundred acres with them. It is the common story: commerce first, the individual last. In New York City a truck can block traffic for half a hour on a cross street while it makes a delivery, but an individual driver illegally parked is quickly caught and fined.

The orientation of both government and university agricultural experiment stations to commercial interests is a puzzling phenomenon. Robert Rudd in *Pesticides and the Living*

Landscape noted in his discussion of control of rodents on government-administered grazing lands in the West that no experiment station seemed to be doing the slightest investigation of the long-term effects of control programs on the ecology of the areas. Certainly the same can be said now for the experiment stations which deal with fruit. Not only is their work on new varieties of apples directed toward varieties that will enable the commercial orchardist to make more money, rather than toward a finer tasting apple, but their recommendations for control of pests in apple orchards seem to ignore completely the possible long-term effects of their recommended spray programs, not only upon the ecology of the areas involved, but of all adjacent lands and of the whole watershed into which the orchards drain.

In the fruit experiment stations the powers behind the throne are not quite so much the growers of apples, but the various companies that manufacture the chemicals which the stations recommend. The stations seem to leave it up to the scientists employed by the oil and chemical firms to do the investigation and take their word for it. Naturally, a scientist employed by a manufacturer is going to soft-pedal any dangers of the company's products. One might assume a certain influence of big money in legislative circles, but it is harder to stomach that power in the universities. If the centers of learning and research cannot be our safeguards, who can be? Must we assume cynically that since the chemical firms are all too apt to give scholarships, the university administrations hate to offend?

There is no doubt that fruit orchards are danger spots. Clive A. Edwards in the 1973 edition of *Persistent Pesticides in the Environment,* a conservative book in its treatment of the dangers of pesticides, gives a table of the residues of DDT and related compounds in soils in the United States tested between 1950 and 1971. A summary of ten tests made in orchards gives an average maximum of 85.0 pp10^6 and an average mean of 42.4, as against an average from ten other agricultural soils of a maximum of 25.6 and an average mean of 4.7. The orchard soils are drenched in chemicals. Edwards also estimates that since the beginning of their use, more than a million and one-quarter tons of DDT have been manufactured in the United States, and three-quarters of a million tons of aldrin and dieldrin. Though the ban upon their use increases, all of them are still being exported in large quantities to underdeveloped nations.

New discoveries and new claims come each year of pesticides that do not persist but are rapidly degraded both in soil and water. New York State at the moment seems to have settled upon Sevin and methoxychlor as safe. Now, Sevin is one of the carbamates, and what experiments have been made with it show that it does degrade rather rapidly in the soil. The only note I can find on its toxicity, except its dangers to man given in warnings on the package, is that it kills earthworms. Nobody seems to have investigated further. Methoxyclor is, one might say, a blood brother to DDT. Its molecule is almost identical except that it has one less chlorine atom than the molecule of DDT. It also kills earthworms. I can find no other reports on its toxicity. So the best one can say so far is that the advance remains only one step ahead of the undertaker, that the new chemicals are only a little less dangerous than the old but still dangerous. In the meantime, the number of commercial orchards increases, the resistance of pests to the insecticides increases, and the unknown dangers to the future loom more ominous. What way are we going?

There is no use deluding ourselves with the sure prospect of a safer future. We must face the fact that the commercial production of wormless and scabless apples as practiced in the United States cannot succeed without the intensive use of poisons, either organic or inorganic. The chances of success can be estimated from the experience of A. P. Thompson of Front Royal, Virginia, who has actually been growing apples without insecticides or fungicides for the past twenty-five years. Starting an orchard of young trees on a naturally fertile soil and adding large quantities of kelp and fish meal to feed the trees, he has kept an orchard that he calls "biologically grown," all emphasis being upon building and maintaining a healthy living soil. His orchard has produced well, but for every bushel of apples suitable for shipping, he reports that five bushels have to be rejected for malformation, lack of good color, fungus spots, or insect damage. About one-half bushel of this five is dumped on the compost pile because of the presence of worms or rot. The remaining four and one-half bushels are pressed for juice or cider.

I applaud Mr. Thompson for a notable effort well maintained, but I cannot believe that without a transformation of humanity the average commercial orchardist in the United States is going to be satisfied with getting top prices for only sixteen percent of his crop.

However, it is a system that has worked in parts of Europe, including France, which is the largest producer of apples in the world. In France, however, the average orchardist is not a one-crop grower. He also keeps livestock, and his apple trees are planted in his pastures. Cows or sheep graze the grass and weeds and, therefore, substitute for the United States' use of herbicides. Since chemicals of any sort would be dangerous to the pastured stock, no spraying with toxic materials is done. At the harvest season the best apples are sold for eating and use in the local markets. The culls are processed for juice, particularly for cider vinegar, which accounts for the largest share of the use of apples in France. I find no records of the percentage of the crop that is salable at top prices, but I assume that it would approximate the percentage that Mr. Thompson gets in Virginia.

Unfortunately, in the United States vinegar is one of the less important by-products of the apple, so that here the economic restrictions of such a system would be more severe.

Of all the chemicals used in the spray programs for apple orchards, the growth regulators and the herbicides have been least tested for their danger. Most of the herbicides are dismissed with a shrug by the experiment stations. Quickly biodegradable, they say, with little more proof than the fact that the soil on which they are sprayed one year will allow some wheat or rye kernels to sprout and grow a month or six months later. Of some of the common fruit growth regulators and fruit drop chemicals, such as Alar (succinic acid 2,2-dimethylhydrazide) or NAA (1-naphthaleneacetic acid), they do not bother to say anything.

For those who find the numbers in the chemical names of organic compounds mystifying, I might explain that a certain number of basic structures are common among most organic compounds. The phenyl ring is an example. It consists of six carbon atoms all connected in what is usually represented as a hexagon. Each of the carbon atoms may have something dangling from it. The numbers in a compound in which a phenyl ring is the base are merely the successive numbers of the carbon atoms in the ring, upon which something new has been added. The same applies to simpler structures like the methanes and the ureas. Occasionally, phenyl rings themselves may join in a more complicated ring, and then the number of basic carbon atoms will go above six.

Frequently, the growth regulators and the fruit-drop controllers are the same chemicals as the herbicides, merely used at different times and in different concentrations. They are all chemicals that in some way or other interfere with, check, or agitate the natural growth functions of plants. Even some pesticides will inhibit plant growth. Now, the basic processes in plants and animals are much alike. The DNA of a plant cell and the DNA of a human cell have the same basic structure. It might logically be suspected that anything which will interfere with the life processes of a plant might under certain conditions and concentrations interfere with the life processes of any animal, including man. It would seem wise that some careful experimenting should be done upon this group of chemicals. To date only a little has been done. This little is recorded in *The Mutagenicity of Pesticides, Concepts and Evaluations* by Samuel S. Epstein and Marvin S. Legator, published by the Massachusetts Institute of Technology Press. A few herbicides are included, but none of the chemicals used solely for growth retardation or growth acceleration.

One of the largest group of herbicides and growth regulators is the series of compounds that are complex phenylacetic acids. In this group belong the herbicides formerly most used, 2,4-D and 2,4,5-T (2,4,5-trichlorophenoxyacetic acid). Both belong to that dangerous group of chemicals in which chlorine has been substituted in the simple phenyl ring. Both were used extensively in the Vietnam War. Experiments at the Bionetics Research Laboratory at Bethesda, Maryland, showed that the ingestion of 2,4,5-T by rats led to fetus deformation, and under the prod of this information, registration of 2,4,5-T was suspended in the United States. Final decision upon permission for its use is still being delayed.

Probably the most used of all herbicides is 2,4-D. Some experimentation has been done on it, but little attention has been paid to the results. Dr. Jacqueline Verrett of the U.S. Food and Drug Administration in a "screening study," found that when 2,4-D was fed to hens, there was subsequent malformation of chick embryos. Another study in the FDA showed that giving 2,4-D orally in large doses to pregnant hamsters showed an incidence of birth abnormalities. Experiments with treatment of root tips of narcissus, *Allium cepa,* and barley anthers show that it produces chromosome aberrations and high abnormal meiosis, that root tips of *Allium cepa* and *Trigonella foreus graecus* in a saturated solution of 2,4-D show C-mitosis and chromosome breaks, and that in rats fed 50–70 mg/kg there is an increase in the frequency of dominant lethals in the sperm. Although 2,4-D is reported everywhere to be quickly degradable, actual experiments show that its persistence in soils depends considerably upon climate conditions, that it is degraded much slower in arid soils, that it can be absorbed by plants and be present, for instance, in the seeds of cotton grown upon soil sprayed with 2,4-D, that its presence has been detected in the milk of cows grazing on pastures sprayed with 2,4-D, and that once it gets into the water of an artificial pond, one of those which now pepper the countryside from Maine to Oregon, it sinks to the bottom and there accumulates for up to two years after its application on nearby land.

Another group of herbicides now much recommended and used is the substituted ureas. In all of them one of the hydrogen atoms of urea has been replaced by a phenyl ring and one or more of the other hydrogen atoms by a methyl group. Diuron is the most used of these, and it seems to lead the Cornell herbicide recommendations under one of its trade names, Karmex. It is 3-(3,4-dichlorophenyl)-1,1-dimethylurea, with two methyl groups substituted and two chlorine atoms added to one of the substituted phenyl rings. All of the substituted ureas inhibit the photosynthesis of chlorophyll, and since photosynthesis is still one of the not completely solved life processes, anything which influences it is interesting to biologists. The reaction in plants of the substituted ureas has, therefore, been studied more than the action of other herbicides. It has been found that they are taken up from the soil by the roots of the plants and translocated to the stems and leaves. Most of the experiments have been to investigate what actually happens in the tissues where photosynthesis is inhibited.

The water solubility of diuron is low, and it, therefore, resists leaching into the soil profile, but stays on the surface, where it may be taken up by plants, or volatilized, or degraded by microbiotic organisms, or adsorbed—stuck on to the outside of soil particles. The soil particles to which it is adsorbed can easily be swept into heavy surface drainage after storms, and so carried to brooks, rivers, and lakes. Degradation in the soil depends upon the moisture content and the composition of the soil. Once the diuron is adsorbed to soil particles, degradation is slower, and this occurs most in moist clay soils rich in organic matter. In such soils diruon has been found to persist more than a year.

In one experiment in which diruon and its related monuron, monolinuron, and linuron were fed to rats, it was found that only twenty to twenty-five percent of the amounts of herbicide administered was excreted in the urine as recognizable metabolites. The major portions remaining were not accounted for. Obviously, the rats did not die, but the report says nothing of toxic effects. I can find only one experiment reported for the mutagenicity of the substituted ureas, and this showed that barley anthers soaked with 1000 ppm monuron or sprayed with 500 ppm monuron both showed abnormal meiosis. What the substituted ureas could in the long run and by accumulation in water, plant systems, or animal systems do to these mediums, no one seems to have paid the slightest attention.

Another herbicide high on the Cornell recommended list is simazine, which belongs to the group known as the s-triazines, built upon a six-membered ring containing three nitrogen atoms. Like the substituted ureas, these inhibit photosynthesis, which means that they too affect a basic life process. Simazine is one of the herbicides most persistent in the soil. C. A. Edwards reported that at the Rothamsted Experimental Station in England, an area of soil treated with a large dose of simazine would not grow any crop for several years. Simazine has also been reported to kill soil organisms. Soaking of barley anthers with 1000 ppm of both simazine and the related atrazine showed a slight effect on meiosis. Beyond this no experiments seem to have been made on its mutagenicity in animals. The only known deaths attributed to herbicides came from eating grain pre-dressed with one of the s-triazines. An incident of this occurred in Iraq in 1973 and resulted in about five hundred deaths and six thousand cases of illness. In quantity, then, the s-triazines are dangerous.

The Cornell list of herbicides for 1978 still includes paraquat, which has for some time been a restricted-use herbicide.

Aside from the possible active danger to animals and man from the intensive use of herbicides, the fact remains that they destroy the natural habitats of underground bacteria and of vertebrates that flourish in the ground and among the grass, weeds, and weed shrubs. On ponds they destroy the plankton upon which fish feed.

In all of the experimentation very little attention has been paid to the possibility of new chemical combinations formed in the soil by the accumulation of not only herbicide residues but of herbicide plus pesticide residues. Many of the complex chemicals are broken down by heat, sunlight, and bacterial action. A complete breakdown usually yields carbon dioxide in the end, but rarely does the degradation proceed to this end. Most of the phenyl, methyl, or amyl groups that are the first steps in the breakdown are active chemical units. What are the possibilities of their recombination into even more toxic compounds? I have seen no mention of experiments to discover this, but it is known that aldrin, a dangerous pesticide, now much banned, is transformed in the soil into dieldrin, an even more toxic and persistent pesticide.

Of all the chemicals sprayed upon apple orchards, I can find least excuse for the herbicides. The excuse given for their use is that it is more economical to kill weeds with a spray than to cut them off with a mowing machine. This excuse may have validity in field crops like cotton or corn, which would require hand weeding, but not much validity for the open spaces around apple trees. Even granted the saving of money for the commercial producer, just how much value can we put upon saving money for the commercial producer if the money saved by him endangers the future of the persons around him? How long are we going to coddle our money-making big brothers at the expense of ourselves?

It is time that we took stock of the mechanical and chemical advances in our culture. Dishwashers save work for the housewife, but they waste water, which may become one of the crucial wastes in a future crowded with too many persons in a drainage area. The automobile and the airplane already show the danger to which they are leading in the future, their own collapse when the limited supply of petroleum for their propulsion is exhausted, and their defilement of the atmosphere. Trees for fuel can be grown with cultivation. Coal and petroleum cannot be replenished. Once gone they are gone forever. Even trees cannot be grown eventually if the soil is sufficiently contaminated with substances toxic to their growth. Already some soils along the Rio Grande have become almost useless from their accumulation of mere salt after long irrigation. What are the possibilities of contamination by the thousands of tons of chemicals that are dumped yearly into the soil under modern agricultural methods?

I close with one sardonic item. In the United States there are many societies formed by and for persons who are particularly interested in and fond of certain groups of living things. For flower lovers these include the Rock Garden Society of America, the American Rose Society, the American Peony Society, the American Horticultural Society, and many others. For bird watchers there is the Audubon Society, which has done so much in pointing out the dangers of pesticides to birds, and there is the Entomological Society of America, which one might assume is made up of persons fascinated by and fond of insects. Among its listed sustaining associates are the American Cyanamid Company, the Gulf Oil Corporation, the Monsanto Chemical Company, the Shell Chemical Company, and the Velsicol Chemical Corporation.

6. Your Apple a Day:
Its Nutritive & Medicinal Value & How to Get a Good One

You would have a hard time sustaining life for long on a diet of apples alone. Like most fruits they are three-quarters water. Their food energy in calories is low though much higher than lettuce. Their protein and fat contents are almost nil. Their carbohydrate content, due to their sugar and pectins, is relatively high for a fruit and about equal to that of pears or pineapples but not up to that of bananas. They are reasonably high in phosphorus, potassium, vitamin A, and ascorbic acid (vitamin C)—those trace elements or compounds so essential to the life processes—but even for these apples are not as rich as lettuce.

The table below gives the nutritive value of apples as compared with a few other fruits or vegetables and with the staff of life, wheat bread. It is summarized from the tables in

Composition of Foods, 100 Grams Edible Portion

Food	Water	Food energy	Carbohydrate	Phosphorus	Potassium	Vitamin A	Ascorbic acid (Vitamin C)
	percent	calories	grams	milligrams	milligrams	international units	milligrams
apples, raw	85	58	14.5	10	110	90	4
bananas	75	85	22.2	26	370	190	10
string beans	92	25	5.4	37	151	540	12
white bread	35	270	50.5	87	85	trace	trace
carrots, cooked	91	31	7.1	31	222	10,500	6
cherries, sweet, raw	80	70	17.4	19	191	110	10
lettuce	95	14	2.5	26	264	970	8
oranges	86	49	12.2	20	200	200	50
peaches, raw	89	38	9.7	19	202	1,330	7
pears	83	61	15.3	11	130	20	4
peas	81	71	12.1	116	316	540	20
pineapples	85	52	13.7	8	146	70	17

"Composition of Foods," *Agricultural Handbook No. 8,* published by the Agricultural Research Service of the United States Department of Agriculture and revised to 1968. I include only those elements of the apple which are in large enough quantity to be of any value.

It can be seen from this table that the apple is relatively low in nutritive value, even compared to other temperate climate fruits. Part of the nutritive value of the apple lies in its skin, for the food energy value, the vitamin A value, and the amount of ascorbic acid of a pared apple are only 54, 40, and 2. If you want to get a full nutritive value from your apple then, you had better eat it skin and all. One must conclude, from a glance at the facts, that one eats an apple more for the enjoyment of eating it than for any body-building value.

The medicinal value of the apple is more difficult to pin down. That it has been considered of medicinal value for some centuries is without doubt. I have tried to track down the origin of the folk saying, "an apple a day keeps the doctor away," but the nearest to fact that I can find is that it seems to be a gradual transformation of an original remark in one of the tales of the *Arabian Nights* about a sickness being relieved by apples. Here one runs into the same difficulty as in the use of the word "apple" in the Bible. The *Arabian Nights* or *The Thousand and One Nights* existed as a collection of folk and other tales in Arabic before A.D. 1000 but was not translated into any northern language before the 1500s. The earliest translation in French, by Antoine Galland, is full of additions and changes by the translator, and since then there have been various translations into English, each with its own emendations and additions. Now the apple was not a common fruit of Arabia, and whether the word in Arabic that has been translated as "apple" really means an apple or actually refers to another fruit is debatable, for there were actually several Arabic manuscripts. It seems more likely that the word was injected into the story by one of the translators.

"An apple a day keeps the doctor away" is obviously a folk saying that has been passed on in England and America for a couple of centuries. What is its justification? Most authorities are rather vague in their answers. The encyclopedias say no more than that the apple is considered a mild laxative, and certain doctors recommend eating pared and crushed apple flesh to remedy constipation, particularly in infants. On the contrary, I know of one doctor, who in the days before antibiotics, used to recommend cored and crushed apple flesh as a remedy for diarrhea on the theory that the pectin in the apple juice would coagulate the fluid of the bowels. I have talked with various persons who have sworn to the efficacy of each of these opposing uses. Like all words and theories that have been long bandied around by people, the result often ends in confusion and contradiction.

Doctor D. C. Jarvis in his book *Folk Medicine* recommends apple cider vinegar as a remedy for many of the woes of the human body, from sterility to sore throat. He bases his value of apple cider vinegar upon its content of potassium, the lack of which in the body he considers the reason for loss of bodily vigor and, therefore, loss of resistance to many diseases. The apple itself he dismisses merely as a healthy food and concentrates upon the value of vinegar made from the apple. This puzzles me, because according to the tables in "Composition of Foods" both apple juice and apple vinegar have slightly less percentage of potassium per weight than raw apples: about 100 milligrams per gram as compared with 110 milligrams per gram in raw apples. Perhaps the reason for this is the easy availability of apple vinegar, for Dr. Jarvis always carries a bottle of apple vinegar along with him whenever he leaves home for a stay. A glance at the table above also arouses the question of why Dr. Jarvis chooses apples instead of several other fruits which have a higher potassium content. The answer to this probably is that Dr. Jarvis comes from Vermont and bases his book upon Vermont folk tradition, and the apple is, of course, the primary fruit of Vermont.

Anyway, if you want to try out Dr. Jarvis's theories, his prescriptions start off always with one teaspoonful of apple cider vinegar in a glass of water, sweetened if you will with one teaspoonful of honey, not with sugar. For general bodily vigor, for inducing potency both in males and females, and for warding off diseases, he recommends this glassful taken four times a day with meals and before going to bed. For diarrhea and vomiting he recommends one teaspoonful of cider vinegar in a glass of water, one teaspoonful of this mixture to be taken every five minutes, and then a second glassful, this to be taken two teaspoonsful every five minutes. For chronic headaches, for high blood pressure, and for dizziness he recommends the same teaspoonful of cider vinegar in a glass of water taken four times a day. For a sore throat he recommends the same mixture used as a gargle every hour, the mixture to be swallowed after gargling.

I have never tried these treatments, so I cannot vouch for them. I will say, however, that I have found one of his folk remedies efficacious: the use of castor oil applied externally for the removal of warts.

Granted that you want to eat an apple—either for its food or medicinal value or just for enjoyment—what are your chances today in the United States of getting a good apple to eat?

If you live in a large city and have no car, your chances are slim. In most of the United States commercial interests are in control. For the commercial orchardist the essential goal is to make the most money out of a limited amount of land, and at the moment the varieties of apples that are making the most money for their growers are largely inferior varieties. The nearer you live to an apple-growing section, the more chance there may be that your local supermarket may now and then buy small shipments of better varieties from the small orchardists who still grow them. Even this is unlikely because the supermarket manager is always afraid that an uncommon variety will not sell but rot in his bins. The difficulty is that the younger generation does not know a good variety from a mediocre one because there has been no chance to taste the good ones. In many ways we become more and more like sheep. We buy what everybody else is buying. In apples this means the Delicious. If you do live in the middle of a large city and you do know the taste of a good apple and the names of the better apples, the best you can do is to complain to the managers of the supermarkets and the managers of the supermarket chains until they begin to stock their bins with varieties better than Rome Beauties and Delicious. How effective such propaganda by consumers may be is questionable, but it is the only answer I see.

If you have an automobile and live near an apple-growing section, then you have a better opportunity. You can visit local orchards that have stands along the highway and buy up to the limit of your storing capacity apples that fulfill the qualities of being good for eating raw and for cooking. Most long-established, small orchards will have a few trees of Northern Spies, McIntoshes, Rhode Island Greenings, Jonathans, and even perhaps a couple of trees of Spitzenburgs. Canned applesauce made from any of these varieties will keep for at least six months without much loss of flavor. (Applesauce made from Red Astrachans will keep a year without loss of flavor.) Preserving apples for pies is more difficult. They can be peeled, quartered, cored, and frozen. The art of drying apples still survives in sections of the country. I can remember from my childhood the long ribbons of apple flesh hanging in the late fall over the kitchen stove to dry. In our family the art died with my grandmother, but there seems now to be a general revival of interest in it. Dried apples make excellent pies. They are essential to the "Schnitz and Knepp" of the Pennsylvania Dutch.

Each section of the country will have its favorite local varieties, often distinctive tasting, excellent apples. One has to learn these by experience. Ask a country housewife what apples are best for pies, for applesauce, for baking and for eating raw. Then experiment.

If you are fortunate enough to live in the country or even in the suburbs on a property with a large back yard, then the better solution is to plant your own apple tree, or trees. If your space is small, you have two possibilities: to plant two or three dwarf trees of good varieties or to plant one large apple tree of a good variety and later graft other varieties upon it. If your space is very small and you still want more than one variety, then plant one dwarf tree of a good variety and later graft upon it. There are many nurseries that sell dwarf trees already grafted to three or four varieties, but the trouble with most of these is that they are grafted with the same mediocre varieties of the commercial orchards. So if you are limited in space and still want several varieties of good apples, it would be advisable to learn how to graft.

Apples are quite easy to graft. The next chapter gives detailed directions for grafting, but I might say that the best way of all to learn is to get an experienced friend to show you. One essential fact that you will have to get by inquiry is the time for grafting in your area. It will be a short period in very early spring for stem grafting and a slightly longer period in mid-summer for bud grafting. Any attempts made outside of those time limits are a waste of time. If your property already has an apple tree, even a poor one, then by grafting you can establish new and better varieties upon it. You can, if you wish, have in time a dozen different varieties on one tree, a variety to a branch, and successful grafts may begin to bear a few fruits within a couple of years after grafting.

If you have no apple trees growing and are going to plant, then you will find yourself confused by the terms describing stock offered in nursery catalogs. This is particularly true if you are looking for dwarf trees, for then you must know not only the variety of apple you are getting but also the dwarfing stock which the nursery uses in its propagation.

The dwarf apple tree is a product of the twentieth century. It is the offshoot of the population explosion. Formerly, the country dweller or even the small town dweller had a sizable piece of land with his house. Now there are too many of us and not enough land. An apple tree is too large for the average yard, even a backyard. So horticulturists solved the problem by producing dwarf trees.

The theory behind the dwarf apple tree is quite simple. The size to which a tree will grow depends largely upon the size of its root system. Certain forms of native European apples, the Doucin and the Paradise, have a small fibrous root system and lack the deep anchor roots of the ordinary apple tree. To produce a dwarf apple tree, one merely grafts the variety he wishes upon the seedling of such a stock. With time the propagation of dwarf apple trees has gathered complexity, both in the choice of stock upon which to graft and the method of grafting.

Most of the stock used at the moment for propagating dwarf apple trees came out of experiments for developing good stock made at the East Malling Research Station in England. This station has over the years developed a series of rootstocks with varying qualitites of dwarfing and disease resistance. The smallest of the lot is the rootstock called Malling IX. An apple grafted upon a root stem of Malling IX will not grow more than six or eight feet tall and will at maturity produce about a bushel of apples a year. This is the common rootstock now used by nurseries that sell dwarf trees. This stock also has the advantage that the trees begin to bear when very young, often on the second or third year.

However, these very dwarf apple trees have several disadvantages. One is that they do not grow well in poor soils, either soil too heavy or too light. They particularly will not stand drought, so that in a sandy soil that drains quickly, they require irrigation, either by hand or system, even if the soil is well fertilized. A continual heavy hay mulch may help on such soils. Perhaps worst of all, the roots of these dwarfs are brittle in addition to being meager, and the tree is, therefore, poorly anchored in the soil. For safety it needs a support all its life, either a stake or a trellis. The root is also susceptible to fire blight. Infection of a low sucker or spur may pass into the root and kill the tree.

The East Malling Station has developed several other rootstocks that are not quite as dwarfed as Malling IX and are to an extent free of its disadvantages. One of the better of these is Malling VII. It produces a semidwarf tree that is better rooted than a tree on Malling IX but still bears early.

There is also a group of Malling-Merton rootstocks. Of these Malling-Merton 106 has been considerably used for commercial orchards in the Northeast, but experience is beginning to show that it is not as dwarfing as originally claimed. The reason for this is apparent when one knows its history. It is a cross between the Malling dwarf stocks and the

Northern Spy. The Northern Spy itself has been used as a rootstock of regular-sized trees for years, partially because it is immune to the woolly aphis (*Eriosoma lanigera*) and partially because it is an extremely vigorous and well rooted stock. It has been particularly successful in the Southern Hemisphere. It was used in Australia as early as 1890, and it was and is still being used in New Zealand and South Africa. The Northern Spy tree is the largest of all apple trees, and these Malling-Merton crosses are, therefore, the combination of two extremes.

The second method of dwarfing is designed to overcome the disadvantages of the shallow and insecure rooting system of the true dwarfs. Instead of using a dwarfing stock as a root, an ordinary apple seedling is used as a base. On its root system is grafted first of all a scion six to ten inches long of one of the dwarfing stocks, and then a scion of the desired variety is grafted on top of this. The result is a semi-dwarf tree that is better anchored than the true dwarf system but still bears early.

A third method of dwarfing is what in some catalogs is called the spur dwarf. The origin of this is quite different. It comes from what is botanically known as a sport. An apple tree may at any time in its life develop a single branch that differs either slightly or quite profoundly from the rest of the tree. A variety whose fruit is streaked red and yellow, for instance, may develop a branch upon which the apples are all pure red. Such was the history of the Delicious, originally an apple streaked red and yellow, but the present red Delicious originated as a sporting branch upon a tree in New Jersey. What happens is that a mutation has occurred in the growth cells of the bud that started the branch from the main stem of the tree. No one can say what causes such a mutation. Colchicine, a product of colchicum, has been used to produce mutations in many garden plants, and it is known that many kinds of radiation may produce mutations. It is speculated that such sporting on an apple tree may be due to cosmic rays that happen to penetrate the bud. Whatever may be the cause, such a sporting branch is actually a new variety of apple, and may, if propagated asexually, be preserved.

Now, one of the ways in which an apple tree may sport is not in the color or shape of the fruit but in the characteristic growth of the stem. The spur sport is a branch in which the stem is slower growing and thickened, and which tends, instead of developing the usual branching structure, to develop an excess of shorter, thick, side branches, the spurs upon which the blossoms and the fruit of the tree are produced. A tree propagated asexually from such a branch will grow slower, bear more fruit, and bear fruit earlier in the tree's life than the normal variety of the tree, though the fruit itself will be identical. This is the spur dwarf. It produces a tree that on the average is two-thirds the size of the regular tree. This spur dwarf has other advantages besides dwarfing. It has a better branching habit, a greater efficiency of fruit production, and often increased winter hardiness. Unfortunately, so far only a few varieties have produced spur sports. Also it has been found from experience that spur-type trees can in later life revert to normal trees. This has been particularly true of the spur Golden Delicious, though not of the red Delicious.

Most nurseries that sell dwarf apple trees indicate in their catalogs the type of dwarfing used. You must, therefore, select the type most fitted to your purpose. Since there is always the question of the adaptability of each type to different kinds of soils, you would do well to inquire of your local agricultural agent what type of dwarf tree seems to be doing best in your locality.

Another difficulty in purchasing dwarf apple trees for the home orchard or yard is that the varieties offered for sale by many firms are the popular commercial varieties, not those most desirable for home planting. If you are going to have your own apples, you should as far as possible have the best, and the present commercial apples are far from being the best. If you live in a climate where the Northern Spy or the Jonathan or the McIntosh will thrive, I see no reason for your ever planting a Delicious. Most of the five-on-one trees advertised by nurseries at the moment are grafted to inferior varieties. On the other hand, they are varieties, like the Delicious and the

Golden Delicious, that have proven themselves adaptable to a great variety of climates from New York to Mexico and one cannot say that of a variety like the Northern Spy. Once again, it is best to consult your local agricultural agent, particularly if you live in a warm climate.

Since this chapter is primarily directed to the small land owner and not to the commercial orchardist, I will not discuss in detail the soil and the situation where the trees are to be planted. I assume that there is little choice in the matter. You have just this space available, and that is it. If there is any choice at all, avoid frost pockets and poorly drained soil. Apple trees in general are a rugged lot and, unless the soil is too completely soggy, will be apt to survive and bear well in most locations. In the more northern sections, spring is the best time for setting out young trees, as early in the spring as the ground can be worked without packing. Farther south, where there is no heavy winter freezing, they can be set out any time during the fall and winter. Holes should be dug a little larger and deeper than the spread of the roots; all damaged roots should be clipped off, and the plant should be set at the same depth at which it was growing in the nursery, except that in a very light and quickly draining soil the young tree might be set slightly deeper in order to get a quicker development of roots in the lower level. It is better to use the richer top soil for filling around the roots, and if even the top soil is heavy clay, to mix it well with compost or well-rotted manure. If the planting is done in sod, the slightly loosened top sods can be placed close to the lower roots and buried under loose soil above. The rotting sod not only offers fertilizer for the roots but also a layer of soil easily permeated by moisture and nutriments. Once the soil is filled in, it should be pressed down firmly with your feet in order to make sure no air pockets are left and to assure close contact between the roots and the soil. If the tree is set early in the spring, root growth will begin before the top growth.

A layer of mulch, hay, straw, or leaves should be spread around the planted tree and left there for at least a year. The mulch should be drawn a few inches away from the stem of the tree in order to discourage mice from making nests near the base.

It would be comforting to say that with the planting and mulching of the young tree, the difficulties are over, but, unfortunately, this would be only wishful thinking. The bark of young apple trees is a succulent food for many pests that love to eat it. For all the years of its growth the tree must be protected from mice, voles, rabbits, deer, and borers. Rabbit protection of a young tree is easy. Simply keep a circle of chickenwire at least two feet high around the base of the tree at all times. Particularly in winter a rabbit can snip off the top growth of a young apple tree as effectively as a man with a knife. During the winter too protection must be given against mice and voles, which work under the snow and close to the ground. The most effective protection is to wrap one layer of tarred building paper, the flexible kind that is used under house siding, around the base of the trunk and tie it with a string. In warmer sections of the country, fine mesh hardware cloth can be used. In northern sections this is slightly danger-ous for a young tree, since the wire cylinder must be fairly close to the trunk to prevent mice from running in at the top, and there is always danger that in a severe winter the cold wire against the tender bark of a young tree might sufficiently lower the temperature to damage the bark. On a very cold winter I have had a young sweet cherry tree with a trunk four inches in diameter completely killed by fine mesh wire wrapped close to its bark. The upper part of the tree, above the wire, was quite undamaged, but within the cylinder of wire the bark was completely destroyed, and the tree died. Granted, apples are hardier than sweet cherries, but some varieties of apples are winter tender, and there is no use taking a chance. Many bulletins recommend various repellents, dried blood, moth balls, and the latest commercial repellents, but our sad experience at the George Landis Arboretum has been that on a winter with many mice and voles and much snow, no repellent is sure. A starving mouse will eat almost anything and will not be discouraged by any repellent, but we have never had a closely wrapped circle of tar paper penetrated.

By the time the tree is well grown and has developed a thick corrugated bark at the base of its trunk, fine-mesh wire can be used in any climate. As a matter of fact, it is better for absolute safety to keep a circle of such wire a foot or so high around the base of even old trees, for in a winter of high buildup of mice or vole population, I have seen a fifty-year-old apple tree with a trunk two feet in diameter completely girdled to about a foot above the ground and killed.

If the deer population in the area is heavy, it would be best to keep a circle of chicken wire or small-mesh sheep wire somewhat over head high around the young apple tree during winter until it gets tall enough to be above the reach of a deer's mouth. This can be removed in the spring, but late, for even after the grass is growing deer like to graze on the tip shoots of young apple trees. Deer will also nip off the tip shoots of the lower branches of old apple trees, which will include some of the flowering spurs, but this is not a serious destruction. However, if deer are prevalent enough to come into your yard during the winter, then it would be wise to put a circle of heavy sheep wire around dwarf apple trees, high enough and far enough out from the tree that a deer cannot stretch its neck over and reach the flowering spurs. In the long run, deer are not such a menace as either rabbits or mice.

Borers are the most insidious destroyers, because their presence is usually not detected until too late. There are several borers that afflict various parts of an apple tree, but the most dangerous is the round-headed apple-tree borer, *Saperda candida*. The adult is a beetle about three-quarters of an inch long, pale brown above, with two broad white stripes extending the whole length of the body. It lays its eggs on the bark near the base of the tree in June or July. The hatched larva bores into the sapwood, and then works upward deeper into harder wood. It requires nearly three years to attain its full growth, in the meantime eating. Its presence can always be discovered by small piles of sawdust at the base of the tree, under the holes. A minor infestation will weaken a tree; a severe infestation will destroy the cambium layer of bark all around the tree and kill the tree. The first sign that an unobservant person may notice is that his young apple tree, now six feet high, begins to look unhealthy with thin foliage and small leaves. By then it may be too late, for if all of the cambium layer around the tree has been destroyed, the tree will die during the season. So one must always be watching the base of a young apple tree for little piles of sawdust, the telltale signs of borer work.

Unfortunately, even when signs of borers are discovered, eradication is not easy. If the larva has not been long inside, the small section of trunk in which it is working may be cut out with a knife and the borer destroyed. It is sometimes possible to run a piece of flexible copper wire up into the hole and force it on up until the borer is destroyed, but often the tunnel is crooked and the wire never reaches the borer. Carbon disulphide, if obtainable, may be injected into the hole with an eye dropper and the hole is closed with some kind of paste or wax, or a nicotine paste may be forced into the hole. I have sometimes had success in putting the nozzle of an aerosol can of insecticide against the opening of the hole and letting the spray be forced into the hole, but since at the present aerosol cans are suspect, I suggest this with reservations.

Like many pests, borers are easier prevented than destroyed. Before the danger of DDT became determined, we used to protect the flowering crabapples in the arboretum from borers by painting the trunks once a year, in late April or early May, a couple of feet up from the ground with a mixture of the cheapest margarine mixed with powdered DDT dust. It was not a particularly dangerous use of DDT, since the amount used was small. Only a little leaked into the soil, and the beetles killed by it were not ones usually eaten by birds. After the banning of DDT many of the experiment stations advised spraying the base of the tree heavily with parathion, but if you dislike to use dangerous chemicals, beware of parathion, which is one of the most toxic of the organophosphates. If you do not mind using chemicals, ask your local extension agricultural agent what is at the moment being recommended as within the law. That the problem is still unsolved is evidenced by the fact that neither of the two spray guides noted in Chapter 5 mention any treatment for borers.

Here at the arboretum we have used with some success a margarine-nicotine sulphate paste painted on the bases of the trees with the paint covered by fine mesh wire so that woodpeckers cannot get to it. If no prevention is used, then one must be continually on the lookout for the telltale sawdust piles and get the young larva out quickly before it gets in too deep.

I realize that the list of cautions and preventions of disaster to your young apple tree is formidable, but when you bite into the first good Northern Spy from your own tree, you will think it was worth all the trouble.

7. Propagation of Apples

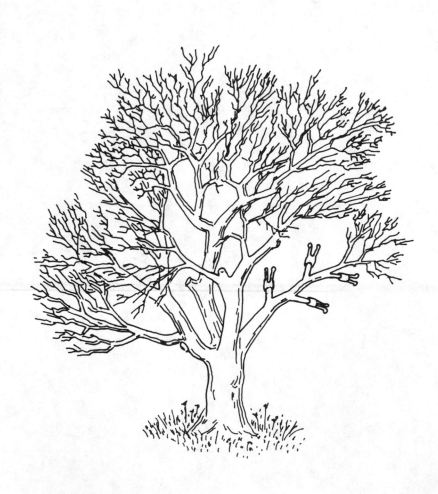

If you are an experimenter or a good horticulturist, you may want to propagate your own apples rather than buying young trees from a nursery. It can be done with reasonable ease. If you start from seed, you must expect that your seedling apple tree will not bear fruit until it is seven years old; furthermore, the chances are slim that your seedling apple will bear as good fruit as its parent. The habit of any species of the genus *Malus* to hybridize with any other species or variety near it and the already complicated genetic history of the modern eating apple make it unlikely that the fruit of a seedling of Northern Spy will bear much resemblance to its parent. Quite likely it will be either too sour or too tasteless to be usable.

Flowering crabapple seedlings, however, often begin to flower before they are seven years old, and a few of the flowering crabapple species, such as the Sargent Crab (*Malus sargenti*) do come reasonably true from seed.

Commercial growers raise apples from seed, usually obtained from cider pomace, the pulp left over after all the juice is pressed out of it. These seedlings are used merely for stock upon which to graft valuable varieties. In the past, seedlings of Northern Spy have been much used for this purpose because of their vigor and hardiness, but now more frequently seeds of a dwarfing hybrid are used. However, the common Merton-Malling stock used for dwarfing has Northern Spy as one of its parents. Commercial grafting is usually done in the winter, when the seedling stock is not more than a couple of years old.

If you want to experiment with seed to see what you can get, the seed should be collected in the fall, as soon as the parent apple is ripe. Sown in the open ground in the fall, where it will freeze over the winter, it will probably germinate the next spring, unless a chipmunk, a squirrel, or a mouse finds it. The danger from these rodents can partially be guarded against by placing a fine-mesh hardware cloth close to the ground over the seed plot and weighing it down with stones. This is not sure protection, for on a deep snow winter any of the rodents may burrow under the edge of the hardware cloth and get the seeds. The cloth should be removed early in the spring, before the germination of the seeds, but even then as much protection as possible should be given against rodents.

A safer but more laborious way is to keep the seeds inside over the winter. In order to get them to germinate the next spring, they should be stratified in moist sand or peat or vermiculite or a mixture of all three. The easiest way to do this is to take an ordinary small plastic flat, the kind in which a dozen annuals are sold in the spring at garden centers, put a piece of newspaper in the bottom to keep the mixture from running out, fill the flat, put the seeds in the top layer of the mixture, and set the flat in your refrigerator for two or three months. If you have only a few seeds, you can bring the flat out of the refrigerator when warm weather begins in spring and put it on the ledge of a cool window, where the seeds should sprout. As they get big enough for transplanting, move them to small pots and in June, to the open ground, or as soon as the soil is workable in the spring, the stratified seeds can be sown directly into the ground, where they should germinate quickly. Again, some protection—such as a tent of hardware cloth over the seed bed—should be given against rodents.

The average home owner, unless he wants to experiment, will not need to take this first step of seed planting. If he has any apple trees on his property or owns an old farm, he will probably have grafting stock already available in chance seedlings that have sprung up in unmowed places. Almost any one of these will make a good base for a future apple tree. Occasionally, one will prove reluctant to make a good union of its bark with the bark of a good variety, and this can only be discovered after a couple of failures to make grafts upon it.

Fortunately, the thick bark of an apple tree makes grafting reasonably easy even for a beginner. The two simplest forms of grafting are scion grafting, in which a small shoot of the desired variety is inserted into the base stock, and bud grafting, in which only a dormant bud of the desired variety is inserted. Scion grafting is done in early spring; bud grafting in midsummer.

There are many forms of scion grafting. In all of them it is

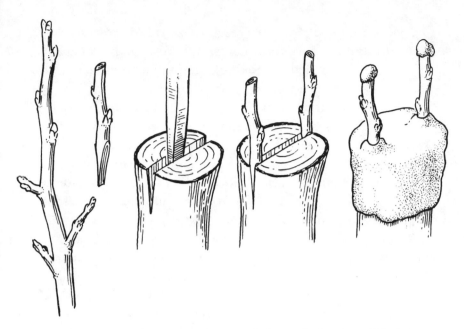

Scion Grafting. *left to right*: End of branch from which scion will be taken. (Only last year's growth is taken.) Section of scion cut and ready for insertion. Cut or sawed off stock split and ready for insertion of scion. Two scions inserted on a fairly large stock. Scions and stock made firm with grafting wax.

important to make sure that the cambium layer of the bark, the inner growing layer, of both scion and stock are carefully matched and then held in place. The easiest method for the beginner is cleft grafting. The success of any good graft depends upon making the graft with a dormant scion at a time when the sap is flowing vigorously in the stock. For cleft grafting, this means a warm day in early spring, but it is important that the scions be taken from the parent tree while their buds are still dormant. Sometimes there will be a warm day in spring early enough to transfer the scions directly from their tree to the grafting stock. Often it is necessary to cut the scions ahead of time and store them in a plastic bag in the refrigerator until a warm day for the grafting arrives. If possible, only the end shoots, last year's growth, should be taken for scions. Second-year wood can be used, but with it the graft is less liable to take.

Cleft grafting can be done on any size stock, from a two-year-old seedling to a vigorous small branch of an old apple tree. The stock, whether the single shoot of a young plant or the branch of an old tree, is either clipped off cleanly if it is small or sawed off cleanly if it is large, care being taken not to lacerate the bark in the process. Then with a sharp but sturdy knife the stock is slit down the middle. There are grafting knives on the market, but good grafting can be done with an ordinary jackknife or even a good kitchen knife if the blade is well sharpened. The slit on the stock is made carefully so that again the bark on both sides of the slit is not lacerated.

The scion is now prepared to be inserted into the slit stock. For this, particularly, the knife blade must be very sharp. Holding the scion firmly in one hand, two slices are taken from it on either side, a little below the bud. Care still must be taken not to lacerate the bark of the scion. The cuts are made so that they join on the back of the scion behind the bud, leaving a wedge-shaped section of scion with clean bark on the front side and a knife-thin layer of wood with no bark on the inner side.

By carefully inserting the knife blade into the middle of the slit in the stock, the stock is gently pried open. A young, small stock splits more easily than an old branch, and with it care must be taken not to pry it too wide, lest it split deeper of its own accord and lose its strength to close tightly over the inserted scion. With the knife tip still in place in the center of the cleft, the prepared scion is pushed down into it up to the top of its cut sides and carefully adjusted so that the barks of scion and stock meet equally along both edges. If the stock is small, only one scion is inserted. If the stock is large, two scions may be inserted, one on each side of the cleft.

The graft must now be protected against drying out and against movement by wind or perching birds. The easiest protection is by grafting wax. This is a combination of beeswax or tallow, which is easily purchased in one-pound blocks. It is hard when cold, but if it lies in the sun, it will soften slightly. The final softening must be done by the hands. The first step is to coat both hands well with petroleum jelly;

otherwise, the grafting wax will stick to every finger. With the hands well greased work off a small wad of the wax and mold it slowly between the palms of both hands until it is malleable. If two scions are inserted in the stock, work the wad into a thin ridge in the middle and carefully drop this ridge between the two scions. Then with the fingers twist one-half of the wax around the base of one scion and the other half around the other, carefully molding it up and around the two scions until all wounds on the stock are covered and the wax is firm around the two scions above the top of the stock, but not covering the low bud on each scion. Smooth the top of the wax over well, leaving no pockets in which rain may collect. During this operation care must be taken not to jiggle the two scions out of their bark-to-bark placement in the stock.

If the graft is going to take, the buds on the scion should begin to expand in a couple of weeks. If they fail, it will be too late to do any more scion grafting that year, but bud grafting can be done in the summer.

Bud grafting, or budding as it is commonly called, is the other type of grafting suitable for apples and usable by the

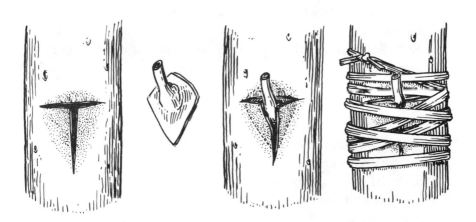

Bud Grafting. *left to right*: Horizontal and vertical cuts made in bark of stock, showing upper ends of bark slightly loosened. Bud, with base of leaf stem left upon it, and cut shield supporting it. Bud inserted in under the two flaps of bark. Inserted bud tightly wrapped with raffia.

home owner. In this method a mature bud of the current year's growth, formed in the axil, or base of the stem of the year's leaves, is inserted under the bark of the stock upon which grafting is to be done. This type of grafting is done in mid-summer. There is a period in the Northeast of the United States about the last two weeks of July or the first week of August, when the next year's buds are already mature and the bark of the stock is still fresh enough that it will separate easily from its under wood.

To gather the buds for grafting, take a vigorous end growth of the summer, cut it off at the base, and put it at once in a plastic bag, so that it will not wilt in the summer sun. If the buds must be gathered at a distance of miles from the stock, the shoots can be stored in the plastic bag in a refrigerator until grafting time.

Once again, the same theory of success applies. The best time is when a good, plump dormant bud can be obtained and the sap is flowing well in the stock. Periods of good sap flow in the summer are usually just after heavy rains.

For stock, either a young seedling apple sapling can be used, or the budding can be done upon a branch of an old tree. In working on an old tree, budding on small branches, not over an inch in diameter, is more successful than on larger branches, because the bark on older branches often does not easily loosen.

With the budding material collected and at hand, the process of budding is as follows. Choose a straight portion of the stock branch, with no buds or side branchlets upon it if possible, and make a T-shaped cut on one side of it. For this again one needs a very sharp knife. The first cut is made horizontally on the branch, about three-quarters of an inch long. In making this cut, the knife should follow the curve of the branch, so that it cuts only through the bark and not into the wood. Then a vertical cut is made, about an inch or an inch and a half long, from the middle of the first cut downward, once again being careful to cut only through the bark and not into the under-wood. Actually, this cut is made most easily by starting at its lower end and working upward to the first cut. At the finish the knife can be turned gently to pry away the two upper flaps of bark. These flaps should be loosened as far down as the length of the backing of the bud to be inserted.

The bud itself is now prepared. On the shoots gathered for bud use, use only the middle buds, for the lowest bud is apt to be poorly developed and the end buds, immature. If you are right-handed, holding the shoot in your left hand, cut with your sharp knife a small shield of bark and bud, which may include a slight bit of the under wood in its middle. Start with the knife blade about three-quarters of an inch below the bud and slowly draw the blade upward under the bud, and surface with the blade about one-quarter inch above the bud. This will yield the bud and shield that are to be inserted in the stock. It will also contain a live leaf. Cut this off, leaving about one-half inch of its stem by which to hold the bud and shield.

Now push the prepared bud gently under the loosened flaps of bark of the cut on the stock until both sides of it are under the loosened bark and its upper end is just below the horizontal cut. In doing this be careful not to lacerate the bark of either the bud shield or the stock.

With the bud in place, all that remains to be done is to tie the loosened bark flaps tightly together over the bud shield. This is done either with a strip of raffia, grafting tape, or a rubber band. All of these can be purchased from horticultural supply houses. If necessary, string can be used but requires more winding and if not carefully wound, may leave puckers along the edges of the bark of the stock, which will let the bud dry out.

In winding, start first with one turn around the top of the cut to hold the bud securely. Then wind downward to the end of the cut on the stock and then back up to the other end of raffia. The same method is used with grafting tape or rubber bands. Strips of rubber can be bought already cut into two- to three-inch lengths. When using rubber bands, the end is secured not by tying but by inserting the final end of the band under the last turn around the branch and then drawing it tight.

Success of the graft can be determined in about two weeks.

If the graft has taken, the bud will remain plump and the stub of leaf stem will still be slightly green. If the graft has not taken, both will have dried and withered. The successfully grafted bud will not grow that season but remain dormant until the next spring, when it will develop into a branchlet. The ties should be cut away in about a month, in order not to constrict growth.

Budding is probably the method more generally used by experienced persons, but I confess that I find it more difficult than cleft grafting in the spring. Perhaps my fingers are too large, but inserting the small bud shield under the bark of the stock and getting it firmly in place without much disturbance of its bark or of the bark of the stock takes some experience.

On a very small stock, say a plant two or three years old, only one bud insertion can be made, and this, if successful, will later become the main trunk of the future tree. In the following spring, after the inserted bud has made its first growth, the top of the stock is gradually cut off. One cut is made first about two or three inches above the growing bud, and the shoot from the bud is loosely tied to this stub for about a month to support the growing bud shoot until its wood hardens. Then the stock is cut off close to the base of the new branch, leaving no stub. The wound will quickly heal over.

On an old tree there is no limit to the number of grafts that can be made, either by cleft grafting or by budding, except that not more than one-quarter of the year's foliage should be removed from a mature tree in one year. An old apple tree of a wild and useless variety can be gradually made over with new grafts made each spring for several years. The tree can be made over either into one variety or into as many varieties as one wishes. Each graft as it matures into a branch will produce the variety of its insert. Grafts will sometimes yield a fruit or two the second year after the graft is made and soon will begin to bear regularly.

One thing to be considered in remaking an old tree is the place upon which to make the grafts. Do not make them on branches low enough ever to get under the snow line on a bad winter, for then mice or rabbits may ultimately eat off all the bark on the grafted branch. Grafts on small stems take more easily than on large stems, so whenever possible graft upon two- or three-year-old shoots coming out of a branch or out of the main trunk of the tree. Gradually, as the graft shoots develop into branches, one must keep trimming out the undesired branches of the stock above them, so that the new shoots always get to the sunlight. One always must be careful not to remove too much foliage from the tree in a single year, or the whole tree may die.

8. The Crabapples

The origin of the word crab applied to an apple is another of the mysteries in the history of the genus *Malus*. The use seems to have started early in England, although the word *krabappel* in Swedish also developed early. In England it seems to have been applied to any small, bitter-tasting apple of the native *Malus pumila*. Where is the resemblance to a crab? It was already commonly used in the 1500s: witness Shakespeare's "When roasted crabs hiss in the bowl . . . ." When Captain John Smith found native apples growing in Virginia with their small green fruits, he called them crabapples. When in the late 1700s the Siberian *Malus baccata* was brought into cultivation, it was called a crabapple, probably because its fruit was so small. When it and *Malus prunifolia* were crossed with common varieties of apples to produce small tart apples suitable for jellies, these were called crabapples. Then in the late 1800s and early 1900s, the many species of *Malus* that were introduced from Japan and China for use as ornamentals were also called crabapples.

Crabapple is a folk term. It has no botanical justification and is, therefore, difficult to pin down. Donald Wyman in *Trees for American Gardens* sets its limits as any member of the genus *Malus* which has fruits two inches or less in diameter, but this would include an old standard variety of eating apple, the Lady Apple. I think I would add to Wyman's definition that the fruit is inedible unless cooked. This would include the idea that has been taken over in an expression like "a crabbed old man." Botanically, most of the species of the genus *Malus* can be called crabapples, for out of the twenty-five or more species, the common or edible apple seems to have developed from only two species, *Malus pumila* and *M. sylvestris,* and some botanists have considered both of these mere varieties of one species. This goes to show how inseparably linked the history of the modern eating apple is with the history of man.

Practically all of the crabapples that are grown for their usable fruit are descendants from two *Malus* species from Manchuria. The most important of these, particularly because of its hardiness, is *M. baccata,* the so-called Siberian Crabapple.

It was introduced to Kew Gardens in England in 1784. It is a large tree, up to forty feet tall, with a spreading head. It has thin branches, light sea green leaves, and large pure white flowers. It is a beautiful tree when in blossom. In late summer it bears small fruit, either yellow or slightly red, less than one-half inch in diameter. From slightly farther east came *M. prunifolia*, a smaller tree, also with large white blossoms and larger and brighter red fruit. By the end of the 1700s it was evident that these two species crossed readily with the standard varieties of apples and that the fruit of many of the crosses made a delicious jelly. These crosses were developed particularly in North America, where the climate was more severe than that of most apple sections of Europe, and it was thought that the hardiness of the Siberian species would develop good eating varieties that would be hardy farther north.

Most of the hybrids proved too tart or too bitter for eating raw, but several soon became standard for jelly making. The Prince Nursery of Flushing, Long Island, was selling a Siberian Crabapple in 1831 and two years later was offering a crabapple called Montreal Beauty, which had been developed in Canada in the Province of Quebec. Most of the varieties of crabapples that became standard were developed along the north edge of apple hardiness, in Quebec, northern Vermont and New York, and particularly in Minnesota, where the hardiness of apples had from the beginning been a problem. The origin of a few of the Minnesota ones is known. Of the common varieties little is known except the first time they appeared in nursery catalogs. They were undoubtably chance seedlings appearing near orchards that were growing one of the Siberian crabapples. Time sifted out the best, and they have persisted to the present. Probably the two most popular were Hyslop and Transcendent. Most farm orchards of the last half of the 1800s contained at least one crabapple tree, and they were even fairly common on small village properties, for the tree was beautiful in blossom, beautiful again when they were covered with the shining red fruit with purple bloom, and their jelly was one of the best. In commercial orchards they never attained much importance, and during the early

1900s, as the old trees died off or got in the way and were cut down, they were rarely replaced with the result that the edible crabapple is not as common today as it was a hundred years ago.

In the early years of this century there was a crabapple tree conspicuous on a lawn of the main street of Esperance, New York. It had grown taller than the house that stood beside it, and its top was a great globe with slightly pendant branches. One of my vivid memories of those years is of that crabapple tree loaded with bright yellow-red fruit and a purple bloom on the exposed side of each fruit, the whole tree like a flaming November sunset. Nothing but a fire ladder would reach to the top of the tree, so the owner had to wait for the apples to fall, and soon the ground under the tree would be as flaming as the top of the tree. The family could never begin to use all the crop, and not being commercially minded, they offered free access to anyone who wanted to make jelly. The Esperance housewives used to come with pails and baskets, like the Biblical women coming to the well, and take the fruit home to make the clear amber jelly that is so delicious on toast for a winter breakfast.

The development of the ornamental crabapples in this century is another of the dramatic sequences that the linked history of the genus *Malus* with man has to offer. It illustrates not only the genetic vigor of the genus but also the cultural lethargy in man which anthropologists have learned to assess as a necessary safety valve in human progress but with which the more farseeing individual is apt to be impatient.

I have already mentioned that *Malus baccata* and *M. prunifolia* were introduced into Europe during the last half of the 1700s. *M. spectabilis* from China was introduced during the same time. All three of these are beautiful in flower.

After this there was a slight lull until the middle of the 1800s. Then two other very important Asiatic flowering species were introduced from Japan, *M. floribunda* into Holland in 1853, and *M. halliana* into the garden of Francis Parkman, the historian, near Boston in 1861.

All three of these trees are beautiful ornamentals. *Malus*

halliana remains still one of the most beautiful on the market. Also it was obvious from the beginning that all would hybridize readily not only with each other but with almost any species of *Malus* except the native North American species, which blossom at a different time. Neither in Europe nor in America did horticulturists or the public pay any serious attention to their ornamental value. They remained merely as individual specimens in arboretums and botanical gardens or occasionally on private estates. By 1883 *M. floribunda* had produced a spontaneous seedling at the Arnold Arboretum, near Boston, which the Arnold thought worthy of preserving, *M. x arnoldiana*, and in 1888 another spontaneous seedling appeared at the Scheidecker Nursery in Germany, *M. x scheideckeri*, with very double flowers. Both of these were an ornament to any garden, but it was fifty years before they really entered the nursery trade and became popular.

About this time an event occurred that was eventually to give impetus to the development of the ornamental crab-apples. In 1891 in western Siberia and Turkestan, a form of *Malus pumila* was found with reddish leaves, reddish flowers, and medium-sized fruit that not only had a red skin but a flesh red right to the core. This was given the unwieldy name of *M. pumila niedzwetskyana*. It is by itself an attractive small tree with red leaves and stems and particularly dark red flower buds. It has, however, liabilities as an ornamental. The dark red flower buds open into flowers that are attractive for about one day only and then, unless the weather is exceptionally cool, fade at once to a washed out magenta, a not very attractive color. The fruits are not sufficiently tasty, either raw or cooked, to be valuable and are large enough to cause a litter problem when the tree is used as an ornamental.

Malus pumila niedzwetskyana showed the usual bent for adventure of the genus *Malus*. It hybridized readily with the newly introduced Far Eastern crabapples. Horticulturists like Lemoine in France quickly saw the value of the red pigment of the variety and began making controlled crosses. In the meantime the collections of Sargent and Wilson from eastern China and Japan had added several new and attractive species, and wherever these were planted they soon showered around a variety of spontaneous seedlings, many of fine horticultural value.

By the turn of the century then, there was available a good selection of ornamental crabapples, all suitable for dooryard, street, or park planting, all crying to be used. Yet it was another twenty-five years before they were much used. I spent from 1917 to 1923 at Cornell University, where with Bailey in the agricultural college one might have expected an early use of trees of such ornamental value. By that time the Colorado blue spruce had already become the status symbol of the small city property owner and a new subdivision of the city of Ithaca, the Heights, had several streets lined with the newly introduced Amur maple, *Acer ginnala*; however, I cannot remember having seen one specimen of ornamental crabapple either at the college or in the city. Twenty years later when the new red-flowered, red-leaved, and red-fruited hybrids like 'Hopa' struck the nursery trade, they suddenly became popular. Now, forty years later they are the common small trees of yards, streets, and city parks. Was it the red that did it? I have already noted the susceptibility of the people of the United States to a bright red fruit. Was it merely cultural lethargy which was finally overcome?

Forsythia, I might point out, was introduced from China and Japan in the first half of the 1800s, yet never became popular until about 1920, after which it spread like a plague over the eastern half of the United States. It is strange to say that the mechanical introductions of our era do not seem to be affected much by this cultural lag. Radio, television, neon lights, Coca Cola, and dispensable cans have spread around the world almost as soon as invented.

In recent years the development of the Oriental crabapples has been so intense and so many new varieties have flooded the market that an individual buying one can scarcely know what to choose. Perhaps because of this, or perhaps from the usual herd instinct to do what everyone else is doing, there has been a tendency to overplant a few varieties and to ignore the better ones.

Undoubtedly it is the red-leaved and red-flowered forms that have been most popular. Since these are all the progeny of *Malus pumila niedzwetskyana*, some suggestions might be offered about their use. First of all, many of them are biennial bearers. They give a profusion of flowers one year and none the next. Secondly, the flowers of even the best of them fade quickly in hot weather, and although some retain their color better than others, most of them tend to look a little washed out after two or three days. About their value in the landscape opinions will vary. At the moment red- and purple-leaved trees are much in favor, as is witnessed by the popularity of the various red forms of the Norway maple, the various red Chinese maples, forms of *Acer palmatum*, the red-leaved plums, and the red-leaved flowering crabapples. Personally, I find that too many red-leaved trees dull a landscape and that they are better used as accents against a background of green. If you decide that you want one of the red-leaved, red-flowered crabapples, assure yourself particularly that the one you are buying from a nursery is an annual bearer. Of those commonly on the market, 'Hopa' is such and probably as good as any. It was developed in 1920 by Niels Hansen at the South Dakota Agricultural Experiment Station as a dual purpose tree. It is good as an ornamental and still has fruit large enough to be used for making jelly. The fruits are about three-quarters of an inch in diameter, dark red and attractive, but not large enough to be a litter problem. The variety *Malus purpurea lemoinei*, developed in 1922 in the Lemoine's Nursery, France, has the darkest flowers of any and holds its color better than most, but it no longer seems to be available from American nurseries. We have in the George Landis Arboretum one spontaneous seedling from this variety which has even darker red flowers, intense red stems, and almost purple foliage, but it flowers sparingly and is a large-spreading ungainly tree. It does, however, show a possibility for future breeding to a well-shaped tree, an annual bearer, but with the same dark red flowers, leaves, and stems. In the present nursery trade these red-flowered varieties are quite mixed up. Many are mere seedlings, their qualities undetermined until they begin to flower. If you want to be sure, buy only grafted stock, and better, see the parent tree in flower and fruit to assure yourself that it is good stock.

To go from one extreme to the other, from dark red to white, there is still no more beautiful white flowering crabapple on the market than the species *Malus baccata*, the original Siberian crabapple. It is at maturity a large tree, as big as a big apple tree, and perfectly hardy. I think there is no purer white among flowers than a spray of *Malus baccata,* and no better background for that white than the light sea green leaves of the foliage at that time of year. The fruits are small and not particularly attractive. They may vary in color from dull greenish yellow to dull reddish green, since many of the original introductions were seedlings and not quite identical, but the flowers and foliage are always the same. Unfortunately the trees tend to be biennial bearers. Here too there is room for future hybridizers: a pure white flowering crabapple (not one which opens pink and turns white) with the light green foliage of *M. baccata*, but a small tree and an annual flowering one. I would welcome such, for certainly a *Malus baccata* in full blossom is one of the gems of a flowering crabapple collection.

There is a whole group of Oriental crabapples with foliage slightly darker than that of the Siberian crabapple and flowers that are rose pink or even red in bud but open to white. Earliest introduced, and perhaps most important of these, is *Malus floribunda*. It can become a tree up to thirty feet tall, but it is fairly slow growing. Its branching habit is dense and the ends of the branches tend to droop. It is particularly beautiful when half in blossom, when the pure white of the open flowers is set off by the dark pink, still unopened buds. Its fruit is small, dull yellow red, and not particularly attractive, but the birds seem to prefer it to that of all the other crabapples. *M. floribunda* is a dependable annual bearer, and it seems to transmit this quality to its seedlings. It has been the parent of several preserved hybrids, particularly of *M. arnoldiana*, which merely seems to have all of the good qualities of the parent intensified. Its rose-pink buds are a little sharper in color, the fruit is slightly larger and more attractive, and the branchlets droop more. We have in our collection one spontaneous seedling of *M. arnoldiana*, probably with an edible apple as the other parent. Its flowers are similar but larger; the branch structure is stiffer and heavier, and the beautiful fruit is about twice the size, the red color of the cheek intensified by a purplish bloom. It is not quite worth preserving, but it shows the diversity still waiting to be explored.

Two others that are somewhat similar are *Malus hupensis*, the tea crabapple, and *M. zumi calocarpa*. Both of these are stiffer branched trees than *M. floribunda*. The tea crabapple is more open in structure with a wide vase shape and long irregular branches. *M. zumi calocarpa* is more dense. Its fruits—small, bright red, and hanging long on the trees—are the more attractive of the two. Both can be depended upon to be covered with flowers every spring with every branch profusely covered with flowers pink in bud but fading soon to white. Their dependability has made them popular for parks and for plantings around commercial buildings, and both are reasonably common in the nursery trade.

Of the light-pink-to-white flowering crabapples the one that seems to me to have been neglected is the first one introduced, *Malus spectabilis*. It was brought from Canton to England in 1780. It used to be cultivated in the Imperial Gardens of China and in temple and private gardens, but it has never been found growing wild, so its origin is unknown. The Chinese always had an eye for things of beauty, and their preservation of *Malus spectabilis* shows it. It is a small tree, tightly vase shaped, with many rigid ascending branches with short thin branchlets. The flowers are like tight double little roses, shell pink, and borne in profusion. They are delicately fragrant. There is something ephemeral looking about the individual flowers and about the whole tree in blossom, the kind of throat catching beauty that is so fragile it seems it might at any moment fade away. Yet, actually, the flowers keep in good condition longer than most. If I were limited to two or three flowering crabapples, one of them would be *Malus spectabilis*. Having been in cultivation and in the nursery trade for a long time, it now appears in several clones, from dark pink to almost white and from tightly double to completely single. The shell pink double form is the most beautiful, but in ordering from a catalog, there is no way of telling what form you are going to get, unless you can visit the nursery and see in blossom the tree from which they propagate. The fruit is small, yellow, and nondescript.

There is one other pink-in-bud-white-in-flower crabapple that is unique along all the other flowering crabapples, *Malus sargenti*, the Sargent crabapple. It was found in 1892 in Hokkaido, Japan, by Charles Sargent, founder and long time director of the Arnold Arboretum. It is a dwarf, rarely growing more than six feet high, and spreads out into an irregular mass of rather distorted branches. It is an annual and profuse blossomer; the flower clusters are quite similar to those of *M. hupensis* and *M. zumi calocarpa*. The fruit is small and bright cinnamon red. It ripens early and is very attractive on the tree long after the leaves are shed.

The flowering crabapple that seems to me to have been shamefully neglected in the United States is *Malus halliana*, sometimes called the Parkman crabapple, after Francis Parkman, in whose garden it first grew. Its botanical name is after Dr. James R. Hall, who sent it from Japan to Parkman in 1861. It has, therefore, been here a long time. It is a widespreading tree with a short trunk and a dense round head with darkish green leaves and long thin branchlets. The flowers are semidouble, cherry red in bud, and bright rose when open, and it fades more slowly, even under heat, than all the other crabapples. Its profusion of blossom and its lack of fading make it for me one of the most desirable of the flowering crabapples. In the George Landis Arboretum collection it is the one most frequently admired. It is not often found in the nursery trade, perhaps because it has a reputation of being the tenderest of the flowering crabapples. However, we have had three specimens in the arboretum for over twenty years, and in that time there was only one year when most of the flower buds were killed during the winter, though the branchlets were not damaged. We expect a temperature of at least twenty below zero Fahrenheit each winter, so that amount of damage in twenty years is slight when balanced against the profuse blossoming of the other nineteen years. However, it should serve as a warning of possible danger in sections farther north, in southern Canada, or perhaps Minnesota. Nevertheless, if I had to choose one flowering crabapple, this would be it.

The varieties that I have mentioned about cover the color range of the Asiatic flowering crabapples and their hybrids, from dark crimson all through the shades of pink to pure white. One other that I always find attractive is *Malus micromalus*, a hybrid between two Asiatic species, probably *M. spectabilis* and *M. baccata,* a cultivated tree of Japanese gardens, introduced into western gardens about 1856. It looks like a small apple tree with a round head, and its flowers look much like the flowers of a Northern Spy apple, but they are borne in more profusion, and they do not fade white but hold a pink cast until they drop. It is the first of all to blossom. I have seen it mentioned as blossoming in alternate years, but the two in the arboretum have always blossomed annually and profusely. The fruit is dull green red, not outstanding in a group, but attractive when looked at closely, a perfectly formed little apple about half an inch in diameter.

I mentioned earlier *Malus scheideckeri*, which presumably was one of a bunch of seedlings from *M. floribunda* crossed with *M. prunifolia*. Its flowers are very double, bright pink, and not as delicate in color as those of *M. spectabilis*, but they are borne in such dense clusters that they cover the tree. It is, however, very slow growing, and one can perhaps get better results by grafting a branch here and there on another tree.

Since all of the European-Asiatic flowering crabapples are such profuse hybridizers, the nursery trade is just now beginning to be full of new and patented varieties. They vary from nursery to nursery, and few of them are available over a wide or general market. Whether they are much better than the old ones is questionable. The tendency seems to have been to select varieties with double flowers and large flowers. It has been the tendency in this century of all hybridizing and selection. We have huge iris, huge roses, huge peonies, and huge black-eyed Susans. Often delicate and graceful form is lost, particularly in the iris. Since profusion of blossom is one of the qualities of the Asiatic crabapples, the size of the individual flower, within certain limits, cannot make too much difference. A branch covered with thousands of small flowers can be as attractive as a branch with fewer larger flowers, and usually increase in size of flowers means decrease in number of flowers.

Among the newer reds, 'Almey', a hardy one out of Minnesota, has become popular. It has red flowers, but the petals are white in the center, a feature more distinctive at close range than at a distance. 'Katherine', an early selection from Rochester, New York, with large double light pink flowers fading white, seems to be coming up in popularity, though sometimes reputed to be a biennial bearer. It is a probable cross of *Malus halliana* with *M. baccata*. At the Princeton Nurseries, at Princeton, New Jersey, 'Almey' was crossed with 'Katherine'. Among the population of seedlings were three so varied and desirable that they have been patented. Of these, 'American Beauty' is red, 'Pink Perfection', pink, and 'Snowcloud', white. All have large double flowers, and according to claim, blossom profusely and annually; however, in 'Snowcloud' no trace of the light green foliage of *M. baccata* remains, so future development in a white is still to be done. Having seen none of these last three, I cannot report from observation on their value.

New hybrids with fancy names are appearing in many catalogs, but unless one can obtain their ancestry or see the tree from which propagation is being made, one can only go by the claims in the catalog. As a matter of fact, seeing a tree in blossom and in fruit is the best criterion by which to select the flowering crabapple you wish to plant. Most of the arboretums and botanical gardens in the temperate sections of the United States now have sizable collections of flowering crabapples. Visit the one nearest you in late April or early May, when they are in blossom, and again in September, when they are in fruit. Choose the ones that suit your individual taste. Then inquire whether the ones you have chosen are annual bearers. Then look for a nursery that stocks the ones you want. It may be that some of them, being spontaneous seedlings that the arboretum has considered worth keeping, are not in the trade. If you want any of these bad enough, go to the arboretum the next March and ask for grafting scions, and graft them on the crabapples you already have or upon ordinary wild apple seedlings, most of which offer compatible stock. A graft on an older tree will often produce a few flowers the next year.

There is one group of flowering crabapples that I have so far ignored, the ones native to North America. If you have driven through western Pennsylvania in late May, you have seen the beautiful masses of pink flowers of *Malus coronaria* dotting the hills, or father west, from Minnesota down the Mississippi Valley, those of *M. ioensis*. These are our natives, which must have come many centuries ago from Siberia to Alaska and down, or perhaps even more remotely down from some more eastern north land mass, when the Greenland area was semi-tropical. There are several species in the eastern United States, only one in the West, and this might indicate the more eastern origin. They are beautiful small trees, more or less round headed in shape, like hawthorns, and their flowers are large, but they are all pink. There is none of the color range of the European-Asiatic crabapples. The fruit is green, rather large for a crabapple, and not attractive on the tree. The early settlers used it for jelly. The American crabapples all blossom about two weeks later than their Oriental relatives.

Only one has ever become common in the nursery trade, the double form of *Malus ioensis*, known as 'Bechtel's Crab,' which was introduced back in 1888 but never became popular until about 1920. It is a beautiful slow-growing tree with very large double flowers of a luscious pink, and though it does not blossom so profusely as the Asiatic flowering crabapples, it is in its own way as outstanding. The flowers are so double that they have lost the ability to produce fruit, but since the fruit would not be attractive, this is no loss. The single-flowered forms make beautiful specimens when in blossom, but if you want one of these, you will probably have to go where they grow wild and collect one, for they are not often in the nursery trade.

These native crabapples have one liability. They are very susceptible to apple rust, a fungus (*Gymnosporangium juniperi-virginianae*) that spends part of its life upon apple leaves and the other part upon the common red cedar (*Juniperus virginiana*). On the red cedar it makes warty knobs that open after a rain into bright orange sponges. On the apple it forms small orange speckles on the leaves, and if there is a severe infestation, can partially defoliate the tree. The damage does not seem to be permanent, but it can occur yearly.

These native crabapples present a slight botanical problem, for as far as I can find out they have never hybridized with any of the Oriental species. There is one hybrid of *Malus ioensis* with *M. pumila*, which seems to have occurred spontaneously in Minnesota, probably near an apple orchard, and another hybrid with *M. pumila niedzwetskyana*, but that is all. This may be because they do not blossom at the same time, but it is easy enough to hold pollen under refrigeration and use it on a later-blossoming flower, and it would seem that some horticulturists must have tried this. When one considers the ease with which the Asiatics hybridize with each other and with the cultivated apple, the barrier between them and the native crabapples plus the later flowering of our natives may indicate an origin nearer Europe than Asia. At any rate, it deserves study. As a matter of fact, the whole group of flowering crabapples needs a botanical overhauling. Several of the Asiatics now commonly given species rank have never been found in the wild and are only preserved in gardens, and they probably are no more species than a Northern Spy apple is a species, merely chance hybrids that have been preserved in clone form. A few of them, like *M. sargenti*, do breed reasonably true from seed, but most of them do not.

All in all, the flowering crabapples are perhaps the greatest gift to man that the genus *Malus* has produced in this century. Like the cultivated apple two centuries earlier, when they found themselves in the climate of northeastern America, they found a climate supremely suited to their growth, and they have flourished and multiplied. They have added tremendously to the beauty of our parks and suburban areas. In the colder sections of the country, where the Oriental cherries are for the most part not successful, the Asiatic crabapples make the most dramatic flowering display of the year, and even farther south they offer a greater range of color than the cherries offer, though the farther south, the greater tendency for the color to wash out quickly. With their fruits in the fall they offer another display, which the cherries do not.

There is only one way to appreciate completely their variety and beauty, and that is to visit a good-sized collection of them in some botanical garden or arboretum or park both in early spring when the trees are masses of red and pink and white flowers and the honey bees are tumbling and humming among them and the air is full of their fragrance and again in autumn when the branches hang loaded with fruits of all sizes and colors, yellow and green and red and purple, and the leaves are falling under the quiet autumnal skies. You may walk away and feel like bowing your head in reverence before the genus *Malus*.

9. The Apple in Europe and Asia

Though all of the eating apples first grown in North America were European, mostly English and French varieties, both the development of new varieties and the method of production soon began to diverge on the two continents and by 1900 had diverged almost completely. It is true that the new American varieties were much exported to the continent and liked there, but they did not in general grow well or ripen well in the European climate and so made little impression upon apple breeding in Europe. In the United States the small farm orchard soon began to give way to the large one-crop commercial apple orchard.

In Europe this shift from small orchards with mixed farming to large commercial plantings has been a development only of this last half of the twentieth century and even now has not reached the stage that it has in the United States. For generations small orchards have been the rule, the large one-crop commercial orchard, the exception. In France, for instance, which has the largest apple crop production in the world (239,699,000 bushels in 1960 as against 105,555,000 bushels in all of the United States), the apple orchards have been small family holdings, part of a mixed farm industry in which the cattle were allowed to graze in the orchards, thereby eliminating weed and grass problems and preventing poisonous sprays. Only the best of the crop was sold on the local markets. The larger proportion of the fruit was used for apple juice, apple wine, and vinegar. The same situation has been in effect through most of central Europe and in Great Britain. Most of the apples in these areas were consumed in the areas where they were grown. Often in these regions the amount of fruit produced was insufficient for the local demand, and in the off seasons apples were imported from Australia, New Zealand, the Argentine, and the United States. A few regions exported apples: Switzerland, north Italy, Yugoslavia, Roumania, and Hungary. Even here the export was mainly to near nations.

In the last few years, however, this situation has been changing. With the need of each country to keep its imports to a low level to prevent an imbalance of money reserve, and with the advent of particularly successful commercial varieties of apples like the Golden Delicious, more and more large orchards are being planted to one or to a few varieties and run simply as orchard industries with no dovetailing of other crops. The size of these newer orchards varies with the climates, the regions, and the exporting facilities. In West Germany and the Netherlands a fruit area of twenty to thirty acres is considered suitable for a livelihood. In the fruit exporting countries the newer orchards are much larger.

In some sections the disadvantage of the small fruit farm has been overcome by having large communal plantings of one variety in which the individual farmer remains the owner of soil, trees, and harvest of one section but in which extensive work, like cultivation, spraying, and often picking, is carried out collectively.

One thing that has changed the picture in Europe is the advent of controlled atmosphere storage. This has increased the preservation year round of locally grown fruit in the fruit-shy areas and thus removed some of the need of apple import.

These current changes in production are reflected in the varieties now being grown. For instance, in the warmer sections of northern Italy and southern France, the Golden Delicious, a most profitable commercial variety, has by far taken the lead over the older European varieties in commercial plantings.

The Europeans never seem to have suffered so severely from the obsession with a bright red apple with which we Americans suffer. Remember the early appeal in England of the Newtown Pippin, an apple with scarcely a trace of red. Most of the apples that have been popular for generations in Europe have had a skin with a base color of green to yellow, often suffused or streaked with a little red.

The varieties that have been grown in Europe are much older than those grown in the United States and have a long history with a consequent long list of synonymous names. In Great Britain the variety Decio, a slightly sweet green apple, is said to have been brought in by the Roman general Ezio in

A.D. 450. The Winter Pearmain can be traced back to Norfolk to the year 1200. The Nonpareil came from France to England in the mid-1500s. The Margaret, also called the Early Red Jeneating, dates from 1665. The Quarrenden, reported a native of Devon but possibly brought from France, was recorded in 1672.

In France several varieties go back to the 1500s: the Nonpareil, the Pigeon Blanc, which may have come from Switzerland, the Rambour Franc, recorded in 1535, and the Reinette Franche in 1510. Early in the next century came the Reinette Gris, the Golden Reinette, which probably came from somewhere else in continental Europe, the Fenouillet Gris in 1608, the Drap d'Or in 1623, and the Fenouillet Rouse in 1667.

Varieties that have long been popular in central Europe, judging from their long list of synonyms, are the Danziger Kantapfel and the Edelboredorfen, which probably came out of Germany in the 1500s. The Gravenstein took one name and kept it. It is thought to have come from Schleswig-Holstein in 1669.

The famous Fameuse strain, now so prominent in breeding work through its descendant, the McIntosh, has a disputed origin. Some authorities claim France, some claim Quebec, and some, upper New York State. If it started in America, the seed was probably from France.

Few of these varieties have been able to maintain their popularity up to the present, but they are in the ancestry of most of the present favorites. Since the name Pippin for a variety of apple came into the United States from the New England settlers, it is not surprising that a Pippin still remains one of the most popular apples in Great Britain. It is Cox's Orange Pippin, which is said to have originated in 1830 from seed of variety called Ribston. It was introduced in 1850 and now has forty-five percent of the total British apple production. By now the Pippin part of the name is forgotten, and the variety is called merely Cox's Orange. It is a medium-sized, rather round apple with skin of a deep yellow washed with orange to bright red and mottled and splashed with carmine. The flesh is yellow and firm, crisp and tender, very juicy, and good both for eating raw and for cooking. It has in the last century been occasionally grown in the United States but has never become popular. It has, however, spread all over Europe and into Australia and New Zealand, where it has become the parent of several new varieties. It is reputed to be difficult to grow in poor soils, but that seems to have had little restraint upon its popularity.

Of the other varieties popular in Great Britain, the Worcester Pearmain, undoubtedly a seedling or sport of the original Pearmain, accounts for twenty percent of the dessert apple production in England. Of the cooking apples, a newer one, Bramley's Seedling, is the most important, with a total of sixty-two percent of cooking apple production. Minor varieties, and ones coming up, are Laxton's Superb, James Grieve, and Tydeman's Early Worcester, the last again out of the Pearmain strain, which has never become popular in the United States. Our Golden Delicious seems to be unsuited to the English climate and has made little headway there.

In France with its warmer climate the Golden Delicious had by 1965 taken over fifty percent of the table apples produced; red Delicious, fifteen percent. Others of importance are Reinette, Reinette de Mans, and Boskoop. Boskoop, a Dutch variety dating back to 1856, has been grown in the eastern United States but has never become popular. It is a large apple, yellow green streaked or mottled with red. Its popularity in Europe seems to have risen in recent years, particularly in the more northern sections, for it seems best suited to a cold climate. In France varieties like Cox's Orange and the Pearmains now play only a minor role, and the many other older varieties are confined to old orchards on small farms.

In Belgium Cox's Orange was for years the most popular variety, but between 1950 and 1965 the newer James Grieve began to replace it. Also in Belgium the newer orchard culture and a desire for export has led to large plantings of Golden Delicious. Here at last the American Spitzenburg strain has reached Europe, for Jonathan has become an important variety, along with Stark's Earliest and the English Tydeman's Early Worcester. This same trio also plays a minor role of production in the Netherlands, but the main varieties there are Golden Delicious, Cox's Orange, and James Grieve. Boskoop is losing out in the country of its origin, but some of its red mutations are being planted, the Dutch evidently succumbing also to the red mania.

In West Germany Cox's Orange still leads by twenty to fifty percent of the production, depending upon the locality. Other important varieties are James Grieve, five to fifteen percent; Goldparmain, five to twenty-five percent; and Boskoop, five to twenty percent. In the southern sections Golden Delicious is being much planted.

In the old areas of cultivation in the South Tyrol of Italy, the main varieties are Jonathan, Gravenstein, and red Delicious, with the red mutations of Delicious coming in rapidly. In the warmer sections the Golden Delicious is now most important.

In Austria the main varieties are James Grieve, Cox's Orange, Stark's Delicious, Golden Delicious, and Jonathan.

The farther north in Europe, the greater becomes the necessity for hardier varieties. In Denmark Cox's Orange accounts for thirty percent of the production. Ingrid Marie, a particularly hardy variety, has been much planted, and in younger orchards Lobo, Stark's Earliest, and Jonathan are leading.

In Sweden the local varieties which have proved their resistance to extended winter cold are still favorites: Akero, Savstaholm, and Ringstad. In the warmer sections of the country, however, Cox's Orange, Ingrid Marie, James Grieve, Lobo, and the American Cortland are still being grown.

As we move eastward into the USSR the picture is completely different. There apples are the most important fruit, but in the first years after the revolution their cultivation was neglected in favor of the more needed grain crops. The first large orchards planted on government and collective farms were part of a mixed farming. It was thought that 250 acres of orchard on a 4500-acre farm would give good results. The plans for many of the farms were to have an orchard large enough to supply the families working on the farm with fruit, and to provide additional income by selling the surplus fruit in the nearby cities.

It soon appeared, however, that the 250-acre orchard on the 4500-acre farm did not give good results, and now the percentage of orchard land has on the average increased, creating farms upon which apples are the main crop, but these are not one-crop farms. Soviet economists now recommend that for each 250 acres of orchard from 75 to 250 acres should be added for field crops. The reason for this is horticultural and is dictated by the climate. Most of the Soviet orchards are planted in sections with cold winters and hot dry summers. In such areas permanent grass cover is difficult to maintain and the soil around the trees must be constantly tilled to keep it aerated. Soviet pomologists are convinced that for such soils a heavy application of farm manure every three-to-four years is the most valuable fertilizer, and in order to assure this supply of manure the orchard must be run with enough farm land beside it to sustain a large herd of cattle. The orchard industry therefore is usually combined with a grain and pasture industry. Some of these farms, however, are enormous. The sovkhoz Agromon near Krasnodar in the northern Caucasus has about 12,000 acres, of which 5750 acres are devoted to fruit trees. The general size now recommended for the fruit-growing areas is from 2500 to 5000 acres.

In order to facilitate work on these large orchards, special machinery has been developed, such as a grafting machine, which works like a lathe and cuts stock and scions so that they can be fitted together with ease. Another recently developed machine is an orchard tree planter, which is a huge plow that first cuts a wide deep furrow into which the trees are dropped and then with special attachments covers the roots of the trees and firms the soil about them. For cultivation of the soil around the trees, disc harrows have been developed with detachable parts that fold out when they come in contact with an obstacle, so that it is possible to work the soil close to the trunks of the trees without bark or root injury.

Two old Russian varieties, both well known outside of Russia, are still favorites: the early Yellow Transparent, which is still grown in all apple growing sections of the world, and the winter Antonovka, famous for its hardiness. In the USSR Antonovka is an early autumn variety in the southern regions and a winter variety in the north. It is a pale yellow cooking apple, sour and very aromatic. The Russians like to eat it raw also, and it is the variety most grown in the north. In the Ukraine a newly developed apple, Reinette Simirenko, a tasty green winter apple, is much grown. Many west European and American varieties are also grown: Goldparmain, Calville Blanche, Boiken, Reinette de Champagne, Cox's Orange, Wagener, Yellow Bellflower, Winter Banana, and Rhode Island Greening, and in the far south, Golden Delicious and the red sports of Delicious.

One method of apple culture unique to the Soviet Union is particularly interesting. This is the development of "creeping orchards" in the far north. In the very cold sections of Siberia, particularly around Krasnoyarsk, the temperature in the winter falls regularly to minus forty degrees Fahrenheit or lower. No large-fruited apple varieties will stand this climate, only the crabapples which are hybrids of *Malus baccata*, the Siberian crabapple. The Soviets have worked out a system of growing large-fruited apples in this region. They plant the young trees at an angle, and as the trees grow, they pin down the branches with wooden pegs, so that as the tree develops it spreads over the ground but never reaches a height of over one meter. The heavy snows of the winter cover these creeping trees completely and so preserve them from injury. They produce fruit annually. More than twenty-five-thousand acres of these creeping orchards are now growing in Siberia.

At the far eastern end of the Europe-Asia continent, the genus *Malus* has now found another new ground, northeast Japan. The history of apple production in Japan is curious. Though most of the Oriental crabapples are native there and have been grown in gardens for centuries, the large edible apple of Europe did not reach Japan until late, about the middle of the 1800s, and even after its introduction its culture dawdled for many years. This may be because Japan, particularly in its more southern sections, has so many varieties of edible fruit.

It was only after the Second World War that an intense interest in apple production started, and now development in the northeast section of Japan is rapid. The two growing sections are Sapporo and Aomori, with Aomori the more important. Here apple production is now a major industry, and the Agricultural Experiment Station of Aomori has been very active in the development of new hybrids. Since the development started late, its time unfortunately coincided with the popularity of the Delicious, so it seems to be with the Delicious that the Japanese have been basing much of their hybridizing. However, other varieties have been used: the Golden Delicious, the Jonathan, and the McIntosh. One variety much cultivated in Japan has a strange history. The Japanese call it the Kokko, but it is an American variety known by various names, such as Ralls, Ralls Janet, Ralls Genet, Geniton, and Gennetin. It was probably a seedling on the farm of Caleb Ralls in Amherst County, Virginia. The variations on the name Genet come in because one historian claimed that the variety was brought from France to President Jefferson by M. Genet, but since that claim was never made until a hundred years after the event, it seems dubious. It is a medium-sized apple, yellowish green mottled or striped with dull carmine, and is described as a subacid apple that is very good for eating raw. It spread south into the Carolinas and westward to the Ozarks but never made much headway in the north and now is almost forgotten in the United States. Perhaps because it was a southern apple and, therefore, better suited to milder climates, it has made its way around the world in sections with milder climates. It has been used as a seed parent both in England and in Australia. In Japan in 1962 it accounted for thirty-nine percent of the total apple acreage and in Korea, fifty percent of the total. The Ralls then is not a variety to be dismissed lightly.

Two other famous strains have shown their staying power in Japan: the American Spitzenburg strain, which through its descendant the Jonathan takes second place in production with twenty-nine percent and the either American or French Fameuse strain, which through the McIntosh is third. But the Golden Delicious and certain strains of the Delicious are coming up.

As usual, when the Japanese do anything, they do it well, and their breeding of apples has been no exception. Some of their hybrids are excellent apples. Mutsu, with Golden Delicious as one of its parents, is a large green winter apple that is showing much promise in western New York State and has now even in places begun to hit the supermarkets. The Aomori Experiment Station crossed Ralls Janet with Jonathan to produce Shinko, a promising variety. Other Japanese varieties are Ohrei and Fuji.

For rootstocks in Japan two native crabapples are much used: *Malus sieboldii* and *M. prunifolia*, var. *ringo*. Besides these, *M. baccata* and seedlings of cultivars are often used. The Doucin and Paradise varieties of *M. pumila* bases of the Malling dwarf series, are also used but not commonly.

In that great stretch of land between the USSR and Japan lies the Chinese Republic, a country in the process of redevelopment. With apples it is, as in Japan, almost a process of new development, for in all the centuries of Chinese history, the large edible apple never attained any prominence. There are, according to Chinese pomologists, twenty species of *Malus* growing wild in China, but all of these except one bear small fruits that are scarcely edible. The species *M. baccata* has, as in the United States, been crossed with the large fruited American and European varieties to produce fruit large enough and sufficiently tasty to be used in cooking. There is a variety of *M. pumila* growing wild in the north and west of China, but unlike the European *M. pumila* it is very stable genetically. Although it has been cultivated in China for many centuries, it has in that time produced only two varieties, and these are very similar. The fruit is roundish, about three inches in diameter, and the flesh is rather dry and sweet but not particularly pleasant to the taste. It ripens early in August and cannot be kept in storage longer than two weeks. It has, therefore, never become a popular fruit.

The large fruited European varieties were introduced into China in the late 1800s, usually from America via Japan. As might be guessed from this route of introduction, the American Ralls became the favorite. It was rechristened in China with the glamorous name of Glory of the Fatherland and as late as 1960 accounted for over fifty percent of Chinese apple production. Other varieties cultivated in the older orchards were Ben Davis, Gravenstein, Summer Pearmain, Grimes Golden, Red Astrachan, and Yellow Transparent. In recent years three other American varieties have come into prominence: the McIntosh, the Golden Delicious, and some forms of the red Delicious.

The cultivation of apple orchards in China differs in many ways from the cultivation in other sections of the globe. The reasons are partially climatic, partially historical. Many sections of northern China have for centuries been dry by nature. All sections have so long been over-populated that they have in times of need been stripped of their natural tree vegetation, and this has aggravated erosion of the soil with the danger of swift runoff after heavy rains. To offset this, the Chinese early developed contour planting and land terracing. Since over-population is still a problem, there is a tendency to feel that no land should be used solely for fruit, but combined with other food-growing crops.

The apple-producing sections are in the north and the northeast, one in the Liaoning Province of southern Manchuria and in Shantung, the other on the loess lands in Shansi, Shensi, and Kansu. Most orchards are located on the plains where the soils are fertile, cultivation is easy, and irrigation is possible. Irrigation is important, since on the loess land there is no ground water.

With the growing need for more rice land, young orchards are now being planted on the steep hill slopes which are not suitable for rice growing. Here contour planting and terracing become necessary. The terraces are stengthened with stones, or in the loess lands, where there are no stones, built up with soil with the outer edges of the banks tilted up. Even on these terraced hills irrigation is necessary. Water is often carried to the tops of the hills in wooden tanks drawn by oxen. Each tree receives one to two hundred liters of water four times a year.

As in Japan, the commonly used rootstocks are seedlings of *Malus baccata* and *M. prunifolia*. Young orchards are always intercropped with soybeans, peanuts, Chinese cabbage, sweet potatoes, millet, or buckwheat. In the fall cover crops are planted and later plowed under for fertilization, but it is in the fertilization that the culture is unique. China is not a cattle land, and animal manure is, therefore, scarce. With China's millions of people, human excrement is plentiful, and it is with this that most of the orchards are fertilized. A small amount of pig manure is available, and in sections near the sea fish meal from the fish industry refuse and also seaweeds are both used.

In mulching too one Chinese practice, stone mulching, is unique on the same theory of western alpine and rock gardens. This mulching is practiced on high elevations and in very dry climates. In Kansu Province an area of over 250,000 acres is mulched with stones. Only a nation with too many people could use stone mulching economically, for most of it is done by hand. Small stones, pebbles, or gravel are brought from the dry river beds and carried sometimes as much as twenty-five miles in wicker baskets on bamboo poles on human backs. The soil around the trees is covered with a layer of four inches of pebbles. This not only prevents evaporation from the soil, but keeps the soil warm by absorbing the sun's rays. It is a time-consuming practice, for since intercropping is practiced in most orchards, each spring the stone mulch must be removed around each plant and later set back around the growing plant. Also each twenty years the mulch must be replaced on nonirrigated orchards, and each five years on irrigated orchards, for in time the soil adheres to the pebbles and their value is lost.

Another labor-consuming task that could be economical only in overpopulated China is the paper bagging of individual apples. The fungus diseases are not so destructive in China's dry climate, but a moth similar to the European codlin moth is most prevalent, and it is against this that the bagging is done. About three to four weeks after the petals have fallen, small bags made of newspaper are placed over each apple that is allowed to develop on the tree and are removed about three weeks before the harvest in order that the fruit may acquire its color.

With the growth of modern technology in the Chinese

Republic, chemical disease and pest control is beginning to replace the old method of fruit bagging, but the excess of population over land will probably for a long time make hand labor still the most economical method of production.

In the far north of Manchuria, around Harbin, the climate is too severe for anything except very hardy crabapples to grow in the open, but here the Chinese have taken over the Russian system of creeping orchards, and the hardy Russian variety Antonovka is being grown in home gardens but not yet in commercial production. Farther south, however, in the still too cold Kirin Province, some very hardy, large-fruited varieties are grown commercially: Wealthy, Haralson, Antonovka, and Grushovica Moskowskaya.

Perhaps because of the wealth of other fruits, the apple has been slow to invade the semitropic regions of Asia, but in the last few years the cultivation of apples has been growing rapidly in Kashmir and the western Himalaya states of India at elevations of from five- to seven-thousand feet in Nepal and in the mountains of central Taiwan. In Kashmir an early variety called Ambri is said to be indigenous. A few European varieties, Early Shanbury, Rymer, and King of the Pippins have been much grown, but recent plantings have been mostly of Delicious and Golden Delicious. In Nepal, Delicious, Golden Delicious, Jonathan, and McIntosh are grown. The growth of apple production in Taiwan is very recent. In the 1950s after the construction of a Cross Island Highway, three farms for retired servicemen were established in the central mountainous section, and peaches, pears, and apples are the major fruit crops on these farms. All of these places are pioneering sections for the genus *Malus* but the future in each place seems to be full of promise.

However, there will also be problems in the future, both in Europe and in Asia. It will be noticed that in all of these sections, cultivation tends more and more toward a one-crop system, and all of these orchards are still in the young stage. The one-crop system depends so far completely upon the intensive use of chemical poisons, and how soon these will become dangerous to the air, soil, and water remains to be seen. Practically all of the areas of Europe and Asia that are high-producing apple sections are much more heavily populated than the apple-producing areas of the United States. Pollution can, therefore, more quickly become a problem. How well the new Soviet orchards will stand up after many years under the present system of cultivation and fertilization remains to be seen. As in all sections of the world, shortage of fuel, difficulty of transportation, and increasing bans upon the use of dangerous chemicals may change the direction of apple production. The future system may be forced toward that now still prevalent in the Chinese Republic, in which a good share of fertilization, protection against diseases and pests, thinning of fruit, and harvesting will have to be done by hand labor.

10. The Apple in the Southern Hemisphere

One of the most remarkable evidences of the vigor and adaptability of the genus *Malus* has been its ability to adjust itself to the change from the north temperate zone to the south temperate zone. This means that it has been able to shift its blossoming season from May to October and its fruit-ripening season from October to March, a complete reversal of its normal growing scheme. Very few genera of trees or shrubs have been able to make this shift successfully, and none, as successfully as the apple.

The start seems to have been in Australia. There apple growing goes back to the time of the first English settlement in 1788. The development was at first slow, but by the 1840s commercial production had already started in Tasmania and in Victoria. This increased during the last half of the 1800s, and by the early 1900s apple orchards were growing in all of the Australian states.

The big production, however, has remained in the more southern and temperate sections of the country: New South Wales, Victoria, and particularly in Tasmania, where the apple is the most important fruit grown.

In the early years most of the apples were grown for local consumption, but soon an export market to Europe, particularly to England, began to develop. This was before the days of electric refrigeration or controlled atmosphere storage, and Australia was able to furnish Europe with fresh apples at a time of year when the quality of storage apples in the north was beginning to decline.

By 1960 the production of apples in Australia had risen to 13,562,000 bushels a year. What is more remarkable is the great number of varieties of apples that have been grown in Australia. A list of the varieties now still grown, prepared in 1974 by R. Ikin of the Australia Department of Health, Plant Quarantine Division, notes over 600 varieties, but this includes some duplication of varieties with synonymous names and some twenty varieties of the always sporting Delicious. It is probable, however, that the list would compare well with the number of varieties still grown in the United States, even including those of which only a tree or two remain here and there in old orchards. The Australians have obviously been ready to try out anything, for the list includes most of the well-known United States varieties like the Northern Spy and the various Pippins and the Rhode Island Greening.

In percentage of production the lead varieties are Granny Smith and Jonathan with Delicious, Golden Delicious, Gravenstein, King Cole, Rome Beauty, and Ballarat trailing.

The variety Granny Smith at the head of the production figures emphasizes another feature of apple development in Australia similar to that in the United States, the appearance of chance seedlings that have become important varieties. Granny Smith was a chance seedling that appeared in the garden of Mrs. Maria Ana Smith in Eastwood, a suburb of Sidney, in the 1860s. Supposedly it is a seedling from French crabapple seeds thrown in the garden, though it is hard to believe this after seeing a Granny Smith apple, which is a large green apple that is big or bigger than a Rhode Island Greening. However, there is no record of the apples that were growing nearby, and the French crabapple seed may have had a complex ancestry. Also one must remember the variability inherent in the long-developed gene pool of the genus *Malus*. At any rate, the apple soon became popular locally, spread all over Australia and into New Zealand, was and is still exported to Europe in large quantities, and now has been planted in many orchards in Europe, even in the north of Scotland. I know of no commercial plantings of the variety in the United States, but it is growing and bearing well in the Agricultural Experiment Station at Geneva, New York. It is interesting that it does grow well in these Northern Hemisphere orchards, where again it has had to reverse its periods of blossoming and fruiting, as did the apples of the north in Australia.

It seems to be one of the versatile varieties that will flourish over a wide climatic range. It is a winter apple. Its fruit is medium to large and dark to yellow green with small whitish flecks on the skin. The flesh is hard, crisp, juicy, and greenish to yellowish white. The flavor is subacid to moderately sweet. It is esteemed both for eating raw and for cooking. From my own small tasting I would say it is better for cooking. It has begun now to invade the supermarkets of the United States, at first in California about 1974, and now in 1978 right here in New York State, one of the centers of apple production in the United States. In June it comes to the supermarkets fresh from the Australian orchards at a time when the New York State apples, even the best of them, preserved even by controlled atmosphere storage, have lost the edge of their flavor.

Two other leading Australian varieties are also local developments: King Cole and Ballarat. King Cole was not a chance seedling. It was raised by R. G. Cole at Lang Lang, Victoria. It is a cross between Jonathan and Dutch Migrone and was first exhibited in 1912. It has many of the characteristics of Jonathan, is even a brighter red, and is more conical in shape. Ballarat, sometimes called Stewart's Seedling, is thought to be a chance seedling of Dunn's Seedling, which itself was a chance Australian variety. Ballarat grew in the garden of another Mrs. Smith at Ballarat, Victoria, about 1900. It is a late winter apple that does not ripen until April. The fruit is large and green–yellow flushed with pink-crimson. It is used mostly for cooking.

Another Australian variety frequently grown is the Abas, a chance seedling found at Shepparton, Victoria, in the 1950s. It is described as being similar to the Jonathan but ripening two weeks earlier. It seems to be gaining in favor. The Crofton, a sweet apple, originated on the property of Joseph Cato, Mount Stuart, Hobart, Tasmania, in 1870 and now seems to have spread well over all of Australia. Other chance seedlings that have come out of Tasmania are Tasman Pride, Geeveston Fanny, Legana, and Democrat. Of these Democrat has been the most successful, and its popularity is growing. The Dougherty, an Australian apple with an unknown ancestry, is now grown throughout Australia. New local ones coming up are the Rokewood of 1951 and particularly one called Sturmer Pippin.

It is interesting to note the importance of the old Spitzenburg strain in Australia through its first descendant, the Jonathan. Other American apples that are still much grown, though not on the leading production lists, are the Northern Spy, the McIntosh and its descendant Spartan, and Stayman Winesap. Also among the popular ones are the European favorite, Cox's Orange, and a late New Zealand apple, Splendour.

The Northern Spy has had one important influence upon Australian apple growing. It has furnished the rootstocks for about seventy-five percent of the apple trees in the country. The reason for this is that the Northern Spy rootstock produces a tree not susceptible to attacks of the woolly aphid. In the north temperate zone, where the winters are severe, the woolly aphid is not a dangerous pest because most of its population is killed off during the winter. In Australia the woolly aphids are able to live over the winter and are, therefore, troublesome. Since trees grown on Northen Spy stock are mostly immune to attack, it has become the standard stock for propagation of varieties. With the current increase of commercial orchards and the trend toward smaller trees, some reduction has been made in the use of Northern Spy stock. The dwarfing Malling–Merton clones from England, being formed by a cross between the original Malling native apple stocks and the Northern Spy, include some aphid resistant clones, and these are being used. Also with the use of organic chemical pesticides, aphids can be kept under control, and, therefore, some of the newer orchards are frequently using dwarf trees grafted on the Malling–Merton 106 stock.

The Australian fruit grower enjoys one advantage over the Northern hemisphere fruit grower in that with the more equable winters, the picking of the fruit is not so urgent. Almost any variety can be picked over a period of two to four weeks without loss of quality, and this is a great advantage in harvesting.

In the early years in Australia the great part of the apple crop was sold as fresh fruit, either on local markets or exported to Europe. In recent years, however, there has been a constant increase in the quantity processed for applesauce, juice concentrates, and cider. At the present about thirty percent of the crop is exported as fresh fruit, about twenty-seven percent is processed, and the remainder is sold for local use. In Tasmania where the apple is one of the main agricultural crops, the greater share of the fruit is exported.

The history of apple production in Tasmania, which is the largest apple-producing state of Australia, is worth recording briefly, for it has had more ups and downs than any other apple-producing section of the world. Its troubles have been both horticultural and economic.

The beginnings were pure pioneer. Settlers went into the forested lands, homesteaded a few acres, and planted potatoes, vegetables, a few farm crops, and a few apple trees. It was first of all a question of food for survival. It soon came to be observed that the apple trees were flourishing better than anything else. By 1830 the eastern coast and the valleys of the Derwent and the Tamar were scattered with small farms in which the apple orchard occupied an overlarge share. The climate seemed particularly favorable for apples, with a long growing season of more than 200 frost free days, much sunshine, and a well distributed rainfall of twenty-five to forty inches a year. Furthermore, none of the pests that were so troublesome to apples in England bothered the apples of Tasmania. The trees grew large but were not well cared for and, therefore, bore irregularly and produced fruit that was seldom of high or uniform quality. The quantity of trees, however, kept up a sufficient supply of fruit yearly. The acreage of apples increased, particularly along the inner valleys, with production concentrated in the Hobart and Launceston areas. Soon Tasmania was exporting apples to the other states of Australia and by the 1850s had begun to export to New Zealand, California, the Pacific Islands, and India.

Shortly after 1850 disaster struck. The codlin moth, one of the worst of apple pests, appeared in the northern sections, particularly around Launceston. It spread rapidly in that section, since nothing was done to check it, and by 1870, the situation in northern Tasmania had become so serious that many of the apple orchards were either abandoned or destroyed. The fruit industry in that section faced complete extinction.

Since the southern sections still remained pest free, apple growing moved more and more to the south. But by 1875 the codlin moth had reached Hobart and the adjacent Derwent Valley areas. The only remaining pest-free areas that remained were in the very far south, the Huon Valley, D'Entrecasteaux Channel, and the Tasman Peninsula. Now these areas saw the same pioneer beginnings as those almost a century before in the north and the inner southern valleys. Small holdings were cleared of eucalyptus trees, and small farms were established with small orchards.

By 1890 the codlin moth had spread over the whole island. Infection of apples had become so serious that the state government was forced to pass a Codlin Moth Act to provide for orchard inspection and for the destruction of diseased fruit. In the meantime, the losses from the moth were beginning to change the methods of apple production. Particularly in the far south, which seemed the perfect apple country, the small ignored family orchard gave way to larger orchards with improved methods of cultivation, pest control, and general orchard management.

With this change production in Tasmania took its second big advance, which continued through the next thirty years. In order to take care of the large crops, new fast steamships outfitted with refrigeration chambers were built. With these collecting fruit from the harbor ports, the export of apples to Great Britain and to Europe increased tremendously.

Then came the period of speculation. Apple land in the south had risen in value by 1900 to 250 pounds per acre, and this stimulated a boom for apple planting again in the north of the island, in the Tamar and Mersey valleys. A good share of this development was plain real-estate speculation. Orchards were started by absentee owners and managed by hired overseers. By 1919 production in these northern sections was much larger than the production in the south, but the production in all sections was still spotty. Mediocre varieties were often planted, and the fruit was marketed unsorted.

In the midst of this boom came the First World War. Most overseas fruit shipments became impossible. Also the too hasty planting of northern orchards in unfavorable spots and the weakness of the absentee ownership and poor management were now showing up in poor production. Not only did expansion in the north cease, but again and again failing orchards were rooted out. By 1923 over 200 acres of orchards on the Tamar alone had been cleared out and turned to other production. Also in the twenty years after the end of the First World War the export market to Europe remained unstable. In 1933, for instance, Australia shipped a record of six million bushels of apples to the United Kingdom and hopelessly flooded the market. After that the government put an end to free trade and instituted a system of voluntary regulation as to amount of fruit, size of fruit, and variety, which is administered by the Australian Apple and Pear Board.

In these later years planting in the northern section of the island has remained stable, but the southern sections have gone on growing with increasing one-crop production and careful orchard management. The Huon Valley is now the apple center.

At present the problems facing apple culture in Tasmania seem largely economic. The expansion of apple production in the western United States, the increase of large one-crop orchards in Europe, and modern methods of keeping apples for long periods, such as controlled atmosphere storage, all have combined to make a dwindling export market. Without an active export market apple production in Tasmania is in danger, for its own population cannot begin to use all the apples grown there.

New Zealand, so near Australia, and with mountains of higher elevation might naturally be thought a better locale for apple development than Australia, but so far it does not seem to have developed as vigorous an industry. Up to 1965 there were few extensive apple orchards in New Zealand, the majority being of ten to fourteen acres, with mixed plantings, mostly family affairs. The main centers of production are Nelson and Hawkes Bay. Around Hawkes Bay yields have reached up to two thousand bushels per acre.

In varieties too New Zealand seems slightly more conservative. The Sturmer Pippin leads with twenty-two percent of production; Delicious, next with fourteen percent; Granny Smith, thirteen percent; Jonathan, eleven percent; and Cox's Orange, slightly less. None of these are locally developed varieties, but one local variety, Splendour, is now being much planted. There are local varieties, but their selection came late. Dillingham Beauty goes back to 1872, and Kapai Red, a sport of Jonathan, appeared in 1920. Telstar came in 1934, and Bledislow Cox, a sport of Cox's Orange, in 1938. Toward the middle of the century, however, local development began to make a mark. From the late forties up to 1960 have come varieties like Red Thorle, Giant Geniton, Jupp's Russet, Widdup, and Willy Sharp. Of these later ones Willy Sharp seems to have made an impression in Australia.

For rootstocks New Zealand uses Northern Spy, Merton 793, and Malling XII and XVI and for closely planted orchards Malling-Merton 106.

Sale and consumption is mostly local, but in recent years there has been some export, even to the western United States.

In South Africa some apples are grown, but the climate is really too tropical for the best apple production. Nevertheless, one variety, Tropical Beauty, originated in Maidenstone, Natal, and was later introduced into the warmer sections of Australia. South Africa used to form one of the good export markets for Australian apples, but in recent years its own production has nearly satisfied its demands.

In the western half of the Southern Hemisphere, the Argentine and Chile are the two great apple producers. Of these the Argentine is by far the greater producer, its total production in 1960 having been 19,047,000 bushels, more than that of Australia. In the Argentine the principal growing sections are the Rio Negro Valley and the delta lands adjacent to Buenos Aires. In Chile production is mostly on the land near Santiago, where the fruit is sold locally. In both countries most of the fruit-producing lands have been in small holdings.

The Argentine has for years exported a great quantity of apples to Europe, particularly to Great Britain. The crop in the Argentine is harvested in March and reaches the northern markets when the local supplies are either exhausted or losing flavor. Brazil has been another export market, taking about one-third of the crop.

Though apples have been grown in the Argentine for a great many years, I can find no records of locally developed varieties. The chief varieties grown now are Delicious, Granny Smith, and Northern Spy.

So far the flowering crabapples do not seem to have spread around so actively in the Southern Hemisphere as they have in the temperate sections of the United States. As might be expected, they have made their way more actively in Tasmania, which has a climate nearer ours, and there a range of selections can be found in gardens throughout the state. In the rest of Australia they do not seem to have made much headway, perhaps because the more equable climate allows a variety of semitropical trees of equal horticultural value, and the flowering crabapples do not find an open niche. Also in milder regions their quick fading habit would be a liability, since many of them, if they opened their flowers in very warm weather, would lose the vitality of their color in a day or so. It is also possible that with the rich genetic reservoir of the genus *Malus*, nonfading varieties may appear in the warmer sections.

11. The Future

What is the future for the genus *Malus* and particularly for the eating apple? It is a good time to ask the question, because at the moment the commercial production of apples seems in a crisis in many places. As I write, the New York State apple growers are holding a meeting to decide what to do about their own oversupply of apples and the dwindling prices offered for them. The apple-growing sections of Australia, particularly Tasmania, are facing severe economic difficulties, brought about according to the estimates of their government departments by the general world oversupply of apples and the remoteness of Australia from the large export markets. It is also a time of crisis for mankind, which is faced by a dwindling fuel supply both for heat and for transportation and by a growing pollution of atmosphere, soil, and water.

Since the development of the apple has been so linked with man throughout its history, the future of the apple seems inextricably entwined with the future of man. Perhaps the present oversupply is only temporary, and the now so feared population explosion will furnish markets for the excess apples. Perhaps man will find another source of power for transportation besides oil or coal. Perhaps man will develop strains of apples that are resistant to both fungus and insect pests, and so the vast quantities of poisons now poured yearly into the soil and air and water will be unnecessary. If all of these things happen, the future for the apple is wide open.

One has to face the possibility, however, that none of these developments will happen. What then? If the various organizations now working toward a stabilization of world population succeed in keeping the number of persons in the world close to the present number, then not much future expansion of apple production is possible. More particularly, if no new power for transportation is found and the dwindling oil and coal supply becomes more and more expensive, then the whole apple industry faces a transformation, for markets will be gradually more and more limited to local markets, and large orchards depending upon export of their product to long distances will be outmoded. If disease- and insect-resistant varieties of apples are not developed or completely safe pesticides discovered, then more and more apple growers will be faced by government legislation against the use of chemicals which are a menace to humanity, and by this too the whole industry will face reformation.

The population and the fuel-transportation problem are beyond the scope of this book. Undoubtedly the population problem will not be solved immediately, so one can say fairly surely that there will soon be enough new mouths to eat the present oversupply of apples, provided apple production does not increase proportionately. The transport problem though works directly against this solution. The feeding of these new mouths from large commercial orchards depends upon relatively cheap transportation, and if atomic power proves too dangerous and no other source of transportation is found, then the future of the large commercial orchard is precarious.

On the problem of pollution there is growing evidence that at least a few agricultural experiment stations are at last awakening to its dangers and exploring how to avoid them. The perfect answer would be the development of strains or varieties of apples completely resistant to fungus diseases and to insect pests. According to Professor Robert C. Lamb of the New York State Agricultural Experiment Station at Geneva, New York, the development of fungus-resistant strains is well on the way, but the development of insect-resistant strains scarcely begun.

In the United States the development of fungus-resistant strains was begun in 1945 by Dr. L. Frederick Hough, then at the University of Illinois. He had noticed that in some plots of unsprayed apple seedlings, half of the plants had been defoliated by apple scab and the rest unharmed. He found that the resistant seedlings were descendants of the ornamental crabapple, *Malus floribunda*. With the assistance of Dr. J. R. Shay, a plant pathologist at Purdue University, Lafayette, Indiana, he began a research project for developing scab-resistant eating apples. The program included not only finding what other species of *Malus* were resistant to scab, but also bringing in scab fungus from all over the world to make sure a species would be resistant to all strains of fungus. They found eight different species of *Malus* that were scab resistant. They also investigated the genetics of the resistance and found that sometimes it was due to a single dominant gene and sometimes due to more than one gene.

Researchers from various agricultural experiment stations in the United States and Canada were drawn into the project. Work at the Geneva, New York, station began in 1949. The project also soon expanded to include resistance not only to apple scab but to other fungus diseases. Spartan, Delicious, and McIntosh, for instance, were found resistant to cedar apple rust. Other varieties were resistant to mildew. For fire blight only moderately resistant varieties have been found: Stark crimson, Delicious, Northwest Greening, and Quinte.

The Geneva station now has five numbered selections ready for testing, and it is growing varieties from other stations that have proved to be resistant to scab: Prima, Priscilla, Sir Prize, Nova Easygrow, and Macfree. None of these have any resistance to insect pests. As for the value of the fruits of these varieties, I can personally speak only for Prima, which I have tasted. It is a large, light to dark red conic apple, early fall ripening, quite good eaten raw, perhaps too mild for good cooking, and probably not a good keeper. I'd give it a better taste than either Delicious or Rome Beauty, now so strong on the commercial markets, so it would seem that there are good possibilities.

Work on insect resistance is going on at Purdue, but according to Professor Lamb has not gotten much further than the preliminary stages of developing methods for testing, which I suppose would include methods of estimating populations of insects, what attracts insects to certain trees, what if anything in the genetic makeup of the apples is repellent to insects, and the life histories of the insects themselves. Once these problems are solved, the next step will be the selection of insect-resistant strains from the crabapples, the developed apple varieties, and wild seedlings. Anyone who has lived near an apple orchard or who has walked in the fall among wild seedling trees in pastures or along woodlot and stream edges must have noticed that in years when the infestation of apple maggot is extensive, the fruit of certain trees is either less affected than the average, or occasionally little infected. One of our local Schoharie County varieties, the Hook, a small green early fall dessert apple, is such a variety. Of the wild seedlings, the fruit is often valueless, but if a tasty apple can be developed from the little and bitter fruit of *Malus floribunda,* anything is possible. One can never discount the genetic variability of the genus *Malus.*

In Australia and New Zealand in an effort to keep down the use of polluting insecticides, there has been a recent development of traps using synthetic sex attractants in order to judge the size of insect populations. This permits less spraying when populations are low. Also experiments are being conducted to find the critical stages in the insect's life cycle, so that spraying may be done at the most effective periods, making fewer seasonal spray applications necessary.

Also in Australia and New Zealand mulch is now being used in place of herbicides to keep down vegetation under and around the apple trees in an orchard. Straw is most commonly used, but spoiled hay, sawdust, and pine bark are also used. This is proving very successful.

Most of the development toward disease and pest resistance is far in the future. It takes years of testing to establish the value of an apple variety for disease and fungus resistance, commercial possibility, and taste. In this century, unfortunately, commercial value has been given too much prominence. With the Delicious definitely leading the parade, and the Golden Delicious coming up, the number of commercially planted varieties dwindles each year. With this the prospect for a good all-around apple for the individual buyer grows slimmer. In 1925 between three and four hundred varieties of apples could be found on exhibition at state fairs in the apple-growing sections, and some growers used to keep just one tree of each of several old varieties just to be able to exhibit the fruit at the fairs. In recent years the number of varieties at state fairs has dwindled to forty or fifty. It is a startling decline in fifty years. Mr. Paul Stark, Jr., of Stark's Nurseries, Louisiana, Missouri, the largest apple nursery in the United States, goes as far as to say that there are now only four or five outstanding varieties in commercial plantings. Extension Bulletin No. 63 of the Geneva Experiment Station lists twenty varieties still being planted in New York commercial orchards but states that the plantings of over half of these are continually dwindling. When one looks at the leading varieties, he might conclude that the average eater of the future must resign himself to an inferior apple.

On the other hand, efforts are being made now in the experiment stations to develop an apple with taste as well as one that will be disease and insect free, and commercially valuable. From the Geneva station has come Jonamac, a cross between Jonathan and McIntosh, with some of the good qualities of both parents. Another good one is Jonagold, a cross between Jonathan and Golden Delicious, a large winter apple colored light scarlet over a yellow ground skin. Perhaps most promising of all is Spigold, a cross between the Northern Spy and Golden Delicious. None of these, maybe, taste any better than either of their two parents, but they are all good apples with commercial possibilities, and they would be an improvement over the present Delicious and Rome Beauty.

It is to be hoped that the experiment stations in the next fifty years will pay a little more attention to taste than they have in the past and a little less to commercial value. There ought to be, in these whole United States, at least one experiment agricultural station devoted to the wants and pleasures of the individual, not to those of the commercial grower. Here, with no concern for the profit possible in each new hybrid or the cheapness of each new pesticide, some time might be spent in developing taste as the most important criterion. Here, utilizing the best of the older varieties such as the Northern Spy or the Spitzenburg and with the ever varied and often unexpected potential of the genus *Malus*, who knows what superb apple may yet appear for the home grower?

In spite of the report of the Geneva, New York, experiment station (given in Chapter 3) of their lack of success in using the original Spitzenburg instead of its descendant the Jonathan in their crosses, the success of the Idaho Agricultural Experiment

Station in getting a good apple, Idagold, by crossing the Spitzenburg with the Wagener, shows that there are still possibilities in the Spitzenburg itself, and I think they should be more explored.

In future considerations the rich genetic pool of the genus *Malus* must be remembered. The Delicious strain itself is proving to be unstable and rich in sporting varieties. One thing that is needed is an apple with the taste of a Northern Spy that will grow well in more southern climates, in the Carolinas, Mexico, California, and South Africa. So far only the milder flavored varieties, not so good for cooking, have succeeded in these climates. It is true that most of the tropical and semitropical fruits are bland in flavor. They lack the sharpness of a temperate climate apple or plum. There is, however, one semitropical fruit, much grown in Mexico, the ciruelo (*Spondias purpurea*), which is as sharp to the tongue as any plum, so there is the possibility of a tropical, sharply flavored fruit. Who knows but that the genus *Malus* may produce another. Practically every good apple of the past has been a chance seedling. So perhaps at the edge of an apple orchard in Watsonville, California, or in the mountains of Queretaro in Mexico, or in the warmer sections of Australia or New Zealand, some day may appear a chance seedling with the flavor of a Northern Spy. When it does, one can ask little more of the genus *Malus*.

In the meantime, those of us who live in the temperate apple-producing regions of the world can only keep on demanding Northern Spies and McIntoshes and Jonathans or their new hybrids in place of Delicious and Rome Beauty.

Source List of
Nursery Stock

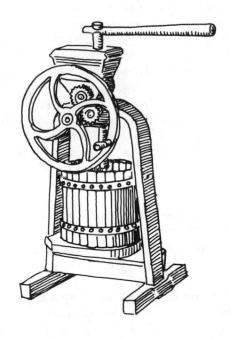

Apple Stock

The list includes nurseries offering at least a few of the older varieties. The starred firms offer the larger lists of old varieties. In general it is advisable to get stock from nurseries in your locality.

*Adams County Nursery, Inc., Aspers, PA 17304

*Baum's Nursery, RD 2, New Fairfield, CT 06810 (The most complete listing of any firm in the United States)

*Bountiful Ridge Nurseries, Inc., Princess Anee, MD 21853

Burpee Seed Co., Warminster, PA 18991 or Clinton, IA 52732 or Riverside, CA 92502

C & O Nursery Co., P. O. Box 116, Wenatchee, WA 98801

California Nursery Co., P. O. Box 2278, Fremont, CA 94536

Carleton Nursery, Rt. 1, P. O. Box 214, Dayton, OR 97114

*Columbia Basin Nursery, P. O. Box 458, Quincy, WA 98848

Converse Nursery, Amherst, NH 03031

Dean Foster Nurseries, Hartford, MI 49057

Frank R. Edwards, Route 2, P. O. Box 1086A, Spruce Pine, NC 28777

Farmer Seed and Nursery Co., Faribault, MN 55021 (Mostly new varieties suitable for the far north; a few old ones)

Farmers Seed and Nursery Company, Faribault, MN 55021

Earl Ferris Nursery, Hampton, IA 50441

Henry Field Seed and Nursery Co., Shenandoah, IA

Grootendorst Nurseries, P. O. Box 346, Lakeside, MI 49116

Gurney Seed and Nursery Company, Yankton, SD 57078

Haley Nursery Company, Inc., Smithville, TN 37166

*Hilltop Orchards and Nurseries, Inc., Route 2, Hartford, MI 49057

Inter-State Nurseries, Hamburg, IA 51640

Kelly Brothers Nurseries, Maple Street, Dansville, NY 14437

Lawson's Nursery, Route 1, P. O. Box 294, Ball Ground, GA 30107

*Henry Leuthardt Nursery, Montauk Highway, East Moriches, NY 11940 (Dwarf trees only)

C. M. Lewis Nursery, 38875 Mentor Avenue, Willoughby, OH (All trees on Malling VII stock)

Earl May Seed and Nursery Company, Shenandoah, IA 51601

Mellinger's Nursery, 2310 West South Range Road, North Lima, OH 44452

*J. E. Miller Nurseries, 5060 West Lake Road, Canandaigua, NY 14424 (Has both Spitzenburg and Smokehouse)

Milton Nursery Co., P. O. Box 7, Milton-Freewater, OR 97862

*New York State Fruit Testing Association, Geneva, NY 14456 (A long and well-chosen list)

H. S. Norlin, 4913 South College, Fort Collins, CO 80521
North American Fruit Explorers, 87th and Madison, Hinsdale, IL 60521
  (Not a nursery but a clearing house for old varieties)
Secor's Nursery, North Ridge, US 20, Perry OH 44051
Stark Brothers Nursery, Louisiana, MO 63353
Sutter's Apple Nursery, 3220 Silverado Trail, St. Helena, CA 94574
Van Well Nurseries, P. O. Box 1339, Wenatchee, WA 98801
*Waynesboro Nursery, P. O. Box 987, Waynesboro, VA 22980
Zilke Brothers Nursery, P. O. Box 8, Baroda, MI 49101

Flowering Crabapples
Starred firms offer large lists
Cherry Hill Nurseries, West Newbury, MA 01985 (Does not ship)
*Eisler Nurseries, P. O. Box 70, Butler, PA (Ships only in truckload lots)
*Fiore Enterprises, Route 22, Prairie View, IL. 66069
Girard Nurseries, P. O. Box 428, Geneva, OH 44041
*Heard Gardens, 5355 Merle Hay Road, Des Moines, IA 50323
Kelly Brothers Nurseries, Dansville, NY 14437
*LaFayette Home Nursery, P. O. Box 1A, R. R. 1, LaFayette, IL 61449
*Mellinger's, Inc., 2310 West South Range, North Lima, OH 44452
*Princeton Nurseries, P. O. Box 191, Princeton, NJ 08540 (Minimum
  order of $50.00)
*Spruce Brook Nursery, P. O. Box 925, Litchfield, CT 06759
Tingle Nursery, Pittsville, MD 21850
Valley Nursery, P. O. Box 4845, Helena, MT 59601
*Weston Nurseries, East Main Street, Hopkinson, MA 01748 (Does not
  ship)

Glossary of Technical Terms

adsorption. The adhesion, in an extremely thin layer, of the molecules of gases, of dissolved substances, or of liquids to the surface of solid bodies with which they are in contact. Thus liquid chemicals may be adsorbed to grains of sand or particles of earth and transported with the sand or earth as it is moved by water.

amyl. A group of atoms of hydrogen and carbon, C_5H_{11}, which acts as a unit in certain complex chemicals.

anther. That part of the stamen, the male section of a flower, that contains the pollen.

asexually. Developed not by a method which involves the union of the male and female germ cells, as in a seed, but by a method which retains the cells unchanged. In plants such methods would be grafting, layering, root division, and root, stem, or leaf cuttings.

axil. The base either of a leaf stem from its branch or of a small branch from a larger branch.

biennial bearer. A plant which bears flowers and fruit only every other year.

biodegradable. Capable of being broken down by living organisms, such as soil bacteria, molds, etc.

biota. The complete animal and plant life of a region.

carbamate. Any salt of carbamic acid, NH_2CO_2H, which in turn is built upon ammonia, NH_3.

chlorophyll. A complex hydrocarbon, the green coloring matter of plants, that enables them by the power of sunlight to transform water and carbon dioxide into complex carbohydrates, mainly glucose, which can be digested by animals. The process is called photosynthesis.

chromosome. One of the small bodies in the cells of any form of life, animal or plant, that gives that form its characteristics and regulates its method of growth.

chromosome aberration. Any unnatural joining or breaking up of the chromosomes of a cell in the mating of male and female cells.

clon (also Clone) A group of plants developed by asexual reproduction from one original plant and therefore identical with the original.

cosmic rays. Rays of extremely high frequency and penetrating power, coming from interstellar space and bombarding the earth's atmosphere.

cultivar. A form of a plant that has been either selected or developed by man and kept unchanged by asexual propagation. It is indicated by single quotes around the name; for instance, the lilac 'Lucie Baltet'.

dominant lethals. Combinations of chromosomes that in each sexual mating produce progeny unadapted to growth and, therefore, infertile seed.

gene. One of the divisions of a chromosome responsible for the development of certain characteristics of the plant or animal.

gene pool. The variant genes in the chromosomes of a species or a population of a species, which allow new combinations in sexual reproduction and, therefore, new developments in the species.

genus (plural genera). An arbitrary classification of either plants or animals ranking between family and species, closely related both structurally and in their line of descent in geologic history.

half-life. The time required for half of the atoms of a radioactive element to become expended.

herbicide. Any chemical used to exterminate some or all growing plants.

inorganic. Not made up of carbon, hydrogen, and oxygen; applied particularly to the metals or their oxides.

loess. An unstratified deposit of loam, ranging from clay to fine sand, believed to have been made mostly by wind.

meiosis. The division of each male and female chromosome into a double of itself, the first step in the formation of a new germ cell as fertilization takes place.

metabolite. Any product of chemical changes in living cells as a result of either replenishing or destroying parts of its protoplasm.

methyl. A group of atoms of carbon and hydrogen, CH_3, which acts as a unit in chemical compounds.

molecule. The smallest portion of a substance which retains chemical identity in mass. A molecule is made up of atoms joined together by physical attraction.

mutagenicity. The change of the makeup of cells caused by external sources, such as radiation or application of chemicals.

mutation. A sudden change in either the germ cells or the cells of certain parts of an organism, which results in a change in the physical or chemical characteristic of either the whole organism or of the part affected.

organochlorides. Compounds in which one or more chlorine atoms have been introduced into the makeup of an organic compound; that is, a compound made up of carbon, hydrogen, and oxygen.

organophosphates. Compounds in which any phosphoric acid salt has been introduced into the makeup of an organic compound.

ovary. In botany, the enlarged portion at the base of the pistil, in which fertilization of the flower takes place and the seeds are formed.

phenyl. A group of atoms of carbon and hydrogen, $C_6 H_5$, which is the basic structure of many organic compounds. It is usually represented as a hexagon with a carbon atom at each point.

phenyl ring. The basic phenyl structure (see *phenyl*) usually represented as a hexagon, but often spoken of as a ring.

photosynthesis. The process by which chlorophyll in the leaves of plants is able by the aid of energy from the sun to transform water and carbon dioxide of the air into carbohydrates, usually glucose.

pistil. The female organ of a flowering plant, consisting of the ovary at the base, in which fertilization takes place and the seeds are formed, a tube leading upward from it (style) to the stigma, and the reception head for pollen.

plankton. The passively floating or weakly swimming minute animal and plant life in any body of water.

pollen. The mass of male cells produced on the anthers of a flower for the fertilization of that flower or of similar flowers on that or on other plants.

scion (also cion). A small detached shoot of a plant used for grafting.

sibling. One of two or more progeny from the same parent.

species (singular and plural). The unit in the arbitrary classification of all forms of life, consisting of individuals closely related by certain characteristics of structure, and which in a population will freely interbreed, producing offspring identical to the parents, but which either by the development of their germ cells or because of geographical separation of populations, will not interbreed with very similar forms. It is a classification impossible to fix down completely.

sport. A bud or a seed variation from the normal, such as a branch of a plant which shows a sudden variation from the normal, or a plant grown from a seed which shows definite variations from the normal. The word is also used as a verb, to sport.

stamen. That organ of a flower which produces the male fertilizing cell in the form of pollen.

stigma. The tip or upper part of the pistil of a flower, which receives the pollen for fertilization.

stock. A plant used as a base upon which another plant is to be grafted.

style. The usually thin tube part of the pistil, which conveys the pollen cells from the stigma down to the ovary.

Bibliography

Andus, L. J., ed. *The Physiology and Biochemistry of Herbicides*. New York: Academic Press, 1964.

Arenson, P. A.; Oberly, G. E.; and Brann, J. L., Jr. *Tree Fruit Production Recommendations*. Ithaca, N.Y.: Cornell University, New York State College of Agriculture and Life Sciences, 1975.

Baum's Nursery. *Fruit Varieties of America and Europe*. New Fairfield, Conn.: Baum's Nursery, 1965–1975.

Beach, S. A., *The Apples of New York*. vols. 1 and 2. Report of the New York Agricultural Experiment Station for 1903. Albany: New York Department of Agriculture, 1905.

Boer, Arie den. *Flowering Crabapples*. Chicago: American Association of Nurserymen, 1959.

Downing, A. J. *The Fruits and Fruit Trees of America*. New York: Wiley and Halsted, 1845 (14th edition 1859).

Earle, Alice Morse. *Old-time Gardens*. New York: The Macmillan Co. 1901.

Edwards, Clive A. *Persistent Pesticides in the Environment,* Second Edition. Cleveland: CRC Press (formerly the Chemical Rubber Company) 1971.

Encyclopaedia Britannica, New York: The Encyclopaedia Britannica, Inc. Eleventh Edition, 1910–1911.

Epstein, Daniel S., and Legator, Marvin S. *The Mutagenicity of Pesticides, Concepts and Evaluations*. Cambridge: Massachusetts Institute of Technology Press, 1971.

Goodhand, W. E. "The Growth and Development of the Tasmanian Pome Fruit Industry." *Australian Geographer,* vol. 8, 1962.

Graham, Frank, Jr. *Since Silent Spring*. Boston: Houghton Mifflin, 1970.

Hoffman, M. E. "One Hundred Years of Apples." *Arnoldia,* vol. 32, no. 3, pages 126–132. Jamaica Plain, Mass.: Arnold Arboretum, 1972.

Ikin, R. *Varieties of Fruit Trees, Berry Fruits, Nuts and Vines In Australia*. Canberra, Australia: Australia Department of Health, Plant Quarantine, 1974.

International Horticultural Congress. *Proceedings of the XVII International Horticultural Congress*. College Park, Md.: University of Maryland, 1967.
Cole, Colin E. "The Fruit Industry of Australia and New Zealand."
Hilkenhaumer, F. "The Fruit Industry in the Countries of the European Common Market."
Kajiura, Minoru. "The Fruit Industry of Japan, South Korea, and Taiwan."
Maliphant, Gordon K. "The Fruit Industries of Latin America."
Muhkerjee, S. K. "Fruit Industry of Southeast Asia."
Pieniazek, S. A. "Fruit Production in China."
Pieniazek, S. A. "Fruit Production in the Socialist Countries of Central and Eastern Europe."

Jarvis, D. C. *Folk Medicine, A Vermont Doctor's Guide to Good Health*. New York: Henry Holt and Co. 1958.

Kearney, P. C., and Kaufman, D. D., editors. *Degradation of Herbicides*. New York : Marcel Dekker, Inc. 1969.

Kenrick, William. *The American Orchardist*. Boston: William Kenrick. 1832. (Second Revised Edition 1835).

Korschgen, Leroy J. "Disappearance and Persistence of Aldrin after Five Annual Applications." *Journal of Wild Life Management,* vol. 35, no. 3, July 1971.

McGraw-Hill Encyclopedia of Science and Technology. New York: McGraw-Hill, 1960, 1966, 1971.

Oberly, G. H., and Forshey, C. G. "Cultural Practices in the Bearing Apple Orchard." *Extension Bulletin 1212*. Ithaca, N.Y.: Cornell University, New York State College of Agriculture and Life Sciences, 1974.

The Palimpsest. Special Edition, July. Articles by H. E. Nichols and B. S. Pickett. Iowa City: The State Historical Society of Iowa, 1966.

Pellett, Ken. "Pioneers in Iowa Horticulture: Jesse Hiatt and the Delicious, 1826–1898." *Iowa Horticulture,* vol. I, no. 4, winter. Des Moines: Iowa State Horticulture Society, 1970

Rehder, Alfred. *Manual of Cultivated Trees and Shrubs*. New York: The Macmillan Company, 1949.

Rudd, Robert. *Pesticides and the Living Landscape*. Madison, Wisc.: University of Wisconsin Press, 1964.

Shaulis, Nelson, and Jordan, T. D. "Chemical Control of Weeds in New York Vineyards." *Extension Bulletin 1026*. Ithaca, N.Y.: Cornell University, New York State College of Agriculture and Life Sciences, 1974.

Sheets, T. J. *Degradation and Effects of Herbicides in Soils*. A paper prepared for the First FAO International Conference on Weed Control. Davis, Calif.: 1970.

Sheets, T. J. *The Extent and Seriousness of Pesticide Buildup in Soils from Agriculture and the Quality of Our Environment."* AAAS Publication 85, 1967.

Sheets, T. J. *Problems in the Persistence of Herbicides*. 8th British Weed Control Conference, vol. 3, 1966.

Smith, Muriel W. G. *National Apple Register of the United Kingdom*. London: Ministry of Agriculture, Fisheries and Food, 1971.

Smock, R. M., and Neubert, A. M. *Apples and Apple Production*. New York and London: Inter science Publishers, 1960.

Smock, R. M., and Blanpied, G. D. "Controlled Atmosphere Storage of Apples." *Information Bulletin 41*. Ithaca, N.Y.: Cornell University, New York State College of Agriculture and Life Sciences, 1972.

"Spray Guide for Tree Fruits in Eastern Washington." *Extension Bulletin 419,* Revised January 1974. Pullman, Wash.: Washington State University, College of Agriculture, Cooperative Extension Service, 1974.

Stark, Paul J. "The Golden Delicious Story." Talk presented at the Golden Delicious Conference at Pennsylvania State University, August 13, 1970.

Stickel, Lucille F. "Organo Pesticides in the Environment." Special Scientific Report. *Wildlife* No. 119. Washington, D.C. 1968.

Terry, Dickson. "The Stark Story." Special publication of the *Bulletin*. St. Louis: Missouri Historical Society, September 1966.

Tukey, Ronald B., and Ballard, James K. *Index of Delicious Strains and Selections*. Pullman, Wash.: Washington State University, 1969.

Upshall, W. H., ed. *North American Apple Varieties, Rootstocks, Outlook*. East Lansing, Mich.: Michigan State University Press, 1970.

USDA. "Establishing and Managing Young Apple Orchards." *Farmers Bulletin No. 1897,* 1967.

USDA. "Composition of Foods." *Agricultural Handbook No. 8,* Revised 1968. Agricultural Research Service.

Whiteside, Thomas. *The Withering Rain*. New York: E. P. Dutton, 1971.

Wilson, Ernest H. *Aristocrats of the Garden*. Garden City, N.Y.: Doubleday Page and Company, 1917.

Way, Roger D. "Apple Varieties in New York State." *Information Bulletin 63*. Ithaca, N.Y.: Cornell University, New York State College of Agriculture and Life Sciences, 1973.

Wyman, Donald. *Trees for American Gardens*. New York: The Macmillan Company, 1951 (Revised Edition 1969).

Wyman, Donald. *Crab Apples for America*. American Association of Botanical Gardens and Arboretums, 1955.

Index